WORLD WAR 2 FACT FILES

# Allied Cruisers

ANTHONY J. WATTS

JANE'S PUBLISHING COMPANY
LONDON · SYDNEY

*First published in Great Britain in 1979 by*
*Jane's Publishing Company*
*Macdonald and Jane's Publishing Group Limited*
*Paulton House, 8 Shepherdess Walk, London N1 7LW*

ISBN 0 354 01201 0

Printed in Great Britain by
Purnell & Sons Ltd
Paulton (Bristol) and London

## Data

Classes and technical data have been arranged in chronological order so that the reader can follow the development of the cruiser within individual navies. The classes have been divided into the two main types of cruiser — Heavy and Light. Details of vessels cancelled under the Washington Treaty limitations have not been included.

The tabular data has been arranged in columns in the following order and relates to the particulars of given classes on the outbreak of war in September 1939, or as first completed (or as designed, if not completed) during the war.
1. Class name; 2. Displacement (standard tons); 3. Dimensions metric (length overall, beam and draught at full load); 4. Dimensions imperial (length overall, beam and draught at full load); 5. Type of machinery/number of shafts and propellers; 6. Designed horsepower/maximum designed speed (knots). (Figures rarely achieved during commission); 7. Radius of action (nautical miles)/speed (knots); 8. Oil fuel (tons); 9. Main belt armour (maximum amidships/minimum ends) in millimetres (inches); 10. Deck armour in millimetres (inches); 11. Turret armour face/sides/roof in millimetres (inches); 12. Magazine armour in millimetres (inches); 13. Conning tower armour in millimetres (inches). The figures quoted for armour protection are the maximum over vital areas and do not cover thinning in a particular area. Details of bulkhead armour etc., are not quoted. 14. Guns and torpedoes — bore in millimetres/calibre (arrangement of mountings where known); 15. Number of seaplanes or floatplanes carried/catapults fitted; 16. Complement.

The technical history is arranged as follows:
1. Name; 2. Builder (the legend for these is given below); 3. Month of first commissioning under country where listed; 4. Fate. Space precludes listing full details of losses. Vessels noted as 'lost' were lost in action with enemy forces. For further explanation of fates see table of abbreviations below.

## List of Builders

| | | |
|---|---|---|
| 1. | Amur Yard (Komsomolsk) | USSR |
| 2. | Armstrong Whitworth (Walker) | United Kingdom |
| 3. | At. & Ch. de la Loire (Nantes) | France |
| 4. | At. & Ch. de St. Nazaire (Penhöet) | France |
| 5. | Beardmore (Dalmuir) | United Kingdom |
| 6. | Bethlehem (Fore River) | USA |
| 7. | Bethlehem (Quincy) | USA |
| 8. | Bethlehem (San Francisco) | USA |
| 9. | Brest Navy Yard | France |
| 10. | Cammell Laird (Birkenhead) | United Kingdom |
| 11. | Chatham Dockyard | United Kingdom |
| 12. | Cockatoo (Sydney) | Australia |
| 13. | Cramp Sbdg (Philadelphia) | USA |
| 14. | De Schelde (Flushing) | Netherlands |
| 15. | Devonport Dockyard | United Kingdom |
| 16. | Fairfield (Govan) | United Kingdom |
| 17. | Federal Sbdg (Kearny) | USA |
| 18. | Fges & Ch. de la Gironde (Bordeaux) | France |
| 19. | Fges & Ch. de la Méditerranée (La Seyne) | France |
| 20. | Galerny Yard (St. Petersburg) | Imp. Russia |
| 21. | Harland & Wolff (Belfast) | United Kingdom |
| 22. | Hawthorn Leslie (Hebburn) | United Kingdom |
| 23. | John Brown (Clydebank) | United Kingdom |
| 24. | Lorient Navy Yard | France |
| 25. | Mare Island Navy Yard | USA |
| 26. | Marti North Yard (Nikolaiev) | USSR |
| 27. | Marti South Yard (Nikolaiev) | USSR |
| 28. | Netherlands Dock & Sbdg (Amsterdam) | Netherlands |
| 29. | Newport News | USA |
| 30. | New York Navy Yard | USA |
| 31. | New York Sbdg (Camden) | USA |
| 32. | Ordzhonikidze Yard (Leningrad) | USSR |
| 33. | Palmers (Jarrow) | United Kingdom |
| 34. | Pembroke Dockyard | United Kingdom |
| 35. | Philadelphia Navy Yard | USA |
| 36. | Portsmouth Dockyard | United Kingdom |
| 37. | Puget Sound Navy Yard | USA |
| 38. | Rotterdam Dry Dock | Netherlands |
| 39. | Scotts (Greenock) | United Kingdom |
| 40. | State Yard (Nikolaiev) | USSR |
| 41. | Stephen (Limehouse) | United Kingdom |
| 42. | Stephen (Linthouse) | United Kingdom |
| 43. | Swan, Hunter & Wigham Richardson (Wallsend) | United Kingdom |
| 44. | Todd (Tacoma) | USA |
| 45. | Vickers (Barrow) | United Kingdom |
| 46. | Vickers-Armstrongs (Barrow) | United Kingdom |
| 47. | Vickers-Armstrongs (Walker) | United Kingdom |
| 48. | Wilton-Fijenoord (Schiedam) | Netherlands |

## Abbreviations

| | |
|---|---|
| A/A | Anti-aircraft |
| AP | Armour Piercing |
| BU | Broken Up |
| Canc | Cancelled |
| CTL | Constructive Total Loss (unfit for further use and scrapped *in situ* or subsequently salvaged and scrapped.) |
| D | Diesel |
| DCT | Director Control Tower |
| DP | Dual Purpose |
| E | Electric |
| ft | feet |
| Ger | Germany |
| GT | Geared Turbines |
| HA | High Angle |
| HE | High Explosive |
| hp | horsepower |
| in | inches |
| kg | kilogrammes |
| LA | Low Angle |
| MC | Marine Casualty |
| mg | machine gun |
| mm | millimetres |
| NA | Not Available |
| Pdr | Pounder |
| QF | Quick Firing |
| RNZN | Royal New Zealand Navy |
| Ret | Returned |
| Sbdg | Shipbuilding |
| Sc | Scuttled |
| shp | shaft horsepower |
| Str | Stricken |
| Sz | Seized |
| T | Turbines |
| TE | Triple Expansion |
| Trf | Transferred |
| TT | Torpedo Tubes |
| UK | United Kingdom |
| USA | United States of America |
| USSR | Soviet Union |
| VTE | Vertical Triple Expansion (Reciprocating) |

# HEAVY CRUISERS

## FRANCE

### Duquesne Class
*Duquesne, Tourville*

Bound by the limitations set by the Washington Treaty Conference the French opted to design their first class of post war heavy cruisers to the maximum limits allowable. Thus the design provided for cruisers of 10,000 tons mounting 8-in (203-mm) guns. By opting for maximum displacement and armament the French found, as did other navies designing heavy cruisers under the Treaty limitations, that they were unable to provide the ships with very much protection.

As with many of their warship designs prepared during this period the French attempted to build ships of exceptionally high speed. Machinery design was one of the highpoints of French naval construction between the wars, and that provided for the *Duquesne* class was no exception. On trials the *Duquesne* recorded a maximum continuous rating of 131,770 shp over her four hour trials to develop a speed of 34.12 knots, the maximum speed at one point being 35.3 knots.

The engines were exceptionally reliable, economical, and robust.

Both ships served until June 1940, when they were immobilised at Alexandria. In 1943 they were re-armed with American assistance, the torpedo tubes, aircraft and catapult being removed and radar and light A/A augmented — two quadruple 40-mm mounts and sixteen single 20-mm being added.

### Suffren Class
*Colbert, Dupleix†, Foch, Suffren**

Although collectively regarded as a single class these cruisers all differed in details. The major difference concerned the armour protection. Although the previous class of heavy cruisers had been fast, powerfully armed ships they did lack adequate armour protection. With the general improvement in warship design especially in the field of gunnery, the French accepted that future classes of heavy cruiser would have to be given better protection, particularly along the waterline belt and in the deck armour. This would obviously entail some sacrifices. Savings in weight in other areas were achieved, but not sufficient to provide the increased armour. If firepower was not to be sacrificed the only remaining major area where weight could be saved to provide extra armour (without breaking the Treaty displacement limits) was in the machinery spaces. Lighter

*Duquesne* in December 1933. *Marius Bar*

*Tourville* in March 1937. *Marius Bar*

*Foch* in March 1933. Note the large cranes for handling the aircraft. *Marius Bar*

*Suffren* in May 1933. *Marius Bar*

machinery was fitted which led to a considerable reduction in horsepower (only 90,000 as opposed to the 120,000 in the *Duquesne* class). However improvements in machinery design generally meant that speed was only reduced by about 3 knots to 31 knots.

The protection was gradually improved in each succeeding vessel, rising from a maximum of 951 tons in *Suffren*, the first of the class to be completed, to 1,553 tons with the last ship in the class, *Dupleix*. Further secondary protection was achieved by siting coal bunkers on either beam abreast the after boiler and engine rooms between the anti-torpedo bulkhead and the belt.

It was intended that these coal bunkers would give the vessels an increased radius of action, and *Suffren* and *Colbert* were fitted with two small coal-fired boilers in addition to the standard oil fired boilers. These, however, were omitted from the remaining two ships in the class, and the space allocated for extra oil bunkerage.

Apart from protection the ships also differed in armament, the last two ships carrying a newly designed A/A gun, a 3.5-in (90-mm) weapon mounted in twin turrets on *Dupleix* and single mounts on *Foch*. The first two cruisers carried the same 2.9-in (75-mm) weapon as the previous *Duquesne* class.

Like all other cruisers light A/A was increased during the war, *Colbert* being fitted with six single 37-mm, four quadruple and two twin 13.2-mm and four single 8-mm. *Foch* and *Dupleix* carried four twin 37-mm, the same arrangement of 13.2-mm as *Colbert* and between three and seven single 8-mm. *Suffren* was rearmed in 1943 with two quadruple 40-mm mounts and twenty single 20-mm, having the aircraft and associated equipment and half her torpedo tubes removed to provide the required space.

*Colbert*, *Dupleix* and *Foch* were all scuttled at Toulon in November 1942 but *Suffren* survived the war and was not scrapped until the late 1960s.

## *Algérie*

The *Algérie* was the last of the French heavy cruisers to be built under the Treaty limitations. Great attention was paid to the hull design of the *Algérie* with the emphasis being to attain the high speed of the earlier heavy cruisers, but on a reduced horsepower. To achieve this freeboard was lowered and the cruiser was designed with a flush deck. The designers were successful in their aims and the *Algérie* maintained a speed of 30.67 knots on her three-hour trial on 66,000 shp (75% power). Four shafts were fitted as opposed to three in the previous classes.

Compared to the *Suffren* class armour was strengthened and generally improved with an anti-torpedo bulkhead extending from the armoured deck to the keel. This was fitted inside the main armoured belt and also enclosed A and Y barbettes. The space between the main belt and the torpedo bulkhead was used as bunkerage (both coal and oil being carried) which provided additional protection.

The main armament was identical to that in the previous heavy cruisers, but A/A capability was considerably enhanced by mounting six twin 3.9-in (100-mm) mounts.

The ship was given additional A/A in 1940–41 (eight 37-mm in two quad mountings and twenty 13.2-mm), some of which replaced the tripod mast. To compensate for the added topweight the aircraft and catapult were removed.

Early in 1942 she was extensively refitted, being equipped with a French designed and built radar. Two more quad 37-mm were also added.

The *Algérie* was scuttled in Toulon when the port was occupied by the German forces in November 1942.

*Dupleix* in April 1934. She carries the new 3.5-inch A/A in twin turrets, one of which can be seen abreast the bridge. *Marius Bar*

*Colbert* in February 1941. Her secondary armament is in single turrets. *Marius Bar*

The *Algérie* with a massive bridge structure similar to Italian cruisers. She is armed with six twin 3.9-inch turrets. *Marius Bar*

## 3 Unnamed cruisers

Three heavy cruisers were authorised in April 1940 as a counter to the German *Hipper* class. They were to be an enlarged and improved *Algerie* type. Length would have been increased and many other improvements incorporated into the design.

Displacement would have been increased by 4,000 tons and with length increased by about 70 ft more powerful machinery and a heavier armament could have been mounted. Triple 8-in (203-mm) turrets in A, B and Y positions were to have been carried, but only three twin 3.9-in (100-mm) A/A would have been fitted. Installed power was to have been increased by 36,000 shp which would have given the ships an extra two knots speed.

Although authorised no orders were ever placed for these cruisers.

| CLASS | *DUQUESNE* | *SUFFREN* | *ALGÉRIE* | *UNNAMED* |
|---|---|---|---|---|
| Displacement | 10,000 | 10,000 | 10,000 | 14,470 |
| **DIMENSIONS** | | | | |
| Metric | 191×19×6.3 | 194×19×6.3 | 186.2×20×6 | 202×21.8×6.2 |
| Imperial | 626¾×62¼×20¾ | 636½×6¼×20¾ | 610¾×65¾×20¼ | 662¾×71½×20¼ |
| **MACHINERY** | | | | |
| Unit/shafts | GT/4 | GT/3 | GT/4 | GT/4 |
| HP/speed | 120,000/33¾ | 90,000/31 | 84,000/31 | 120,000/33 |
| Radius/speed | 4,500/15 | 5,300 (*4,600)/15 | 8,700/15 | 4,200/20 |
| Fuel | 1,820 | 1,800 | 3,186 | NA |
| **PROTECTION** | | | | |
| Main belt | None | 54–60 (2⅛–2⅜) (*50(2)) | 110 (4¼) | NA |
| Main deck | None | 25 (1) | 80 (3⅛) | NA |
| Turrets | 30 (1⅛) | 25 (1) (†30 (1⅛)) | 70–100 (2¾–4) | NA |
| Conning tower | 30 (1⅛) | 30 (1⅛) | 70–100 (2¾–4) | NA |
| | 30 (1⅛) | 30 (1⅛) | | |
| **ARMAMENT** | | | | |
| Guns and torpedo tubes | 8×203/50 (4×2)<br>8×75/60 (8×1)<br>8×37 (4×2)<br>12×13.2, 12×550 (4×3) TT | 8×203/50 (4×2)<br>8×90 (8×1, †4×2) not in *<br>8×75 (8×1) in * only<br>8×37, 12×13.2 (4×3)<br>12×550 (4×3) TT in * only | 8×203/50 (4×2)<br>12×100/50 (6×2)<br>8×37 (4×2)<br>6×550 (2×3) TT | 9×203 (3×3)<br>6×100/60 (3×2)<br>6×37 (3×2)<br>6×550 (2×3) TT |
| Aircraft/catapults | 2/1 | 3 (*2)/1 | 3/2 | 2/2 |
| Complement | 605 | 752 (*773) | 748 | NA |

| NAME | BUILDER | IN SERVICE | FATE | NAME | BUILDER | IN SERVICE | FATE |
|---|---|---|---|---|---|---|---|
| Algérie | 9 | 1934 | Sc 27/11/42 | Foch | 9 | 1931 | Sc 27/11/42 |
| Colbert | 9 | 1931 | Sc 27/11/42 | Suffren | 9 | 1930 | BU |
| Dupleix | 9 | 1932 | Sc 27/11/42 | Tourville | 24 | 1928 | BU 3/62 |
| Duquesne | 9 | 1928 | BU 7/55 | | | | |

# UNITED KINGDOM

## County Class
### *Australia*, Berwick, Canberra*, Cornwall, Cumberland, Devonshire, Dorsetshire, Kent*, London†, Norfolk**, Shropshire, Suffolk, Sussex*

These cruisers, collectively known as the *County* Class, were all designed and ordered during the period of the Washington Treaty. Although ostensibly of one class there were considerable differences between the various units which are usually classed in sub-groups.

*Kent* Group — *Australia, Berwick, Canberra, Cornwall, Cumberland, Kent, Suffolk*
*London* Group — *Devonshire, London, Shropshire, Sussex*
*Dorsetshire* Group — *Dorsetshire, Norfolk*

Like other cruisers built to the strict letter of the Washington Treaty, the *County* Class suffered from attempting to achieve the best possible speed and armament within the displacement restrictions. Obviously there had to be sacrifices, and as with other cruisers this was usually the protection, it being considered that with their high speed, cruisers would attempt to avoid joining action with more powerful adversaries.

To achieve the necessary speed characteristics the *County* Class were designed with a long hull and very high freeboard, the latter being felt necessary to maintain good seaworthiness. As a result the *County's*, with their conventional machinery arrangement exhausting into three funnels, acquired a very distinctive silhouette.

The 8-in (203-mm) guns were carried in a standard centre-line fore and aft disposition in four twin turrets. The secondary battery of 4-in (100-mm) A/A was grouped in single mountings abaft the funnels.

The ships completely lacked side armour, such protection as the displacement limitation allowed to be fitted being worked into deck armour over the machinery spaces to provide protection in the event of air attack. Even so the protection provided was still insufficient to cope with modern aircraft weapons.

During refits carried out in the mid-1930s the ships were equipped with an athwartships catapult abaft the funnels, and a large hangar with high silhouette replaced the after superstructure in certain of the British units. The extent of the refits varied considerably between individual units. As a result the

*Canberra* in 1939. *Authors Collection*

Pre-war photographs of *Cumberland* as completed with short funnels.
*Real Photographs*

secondary 4-in were re-sited amidships abreast the funnels, some vessels being given twin mounts. Two quadruple 2-pdr (40-mm) mountings were added immediately in front of the fore funnel to augment the A/A. Varying alterations carried out during these refits resulted in considerable differences developing even between individual vessels within the sub-groups. Some had extra armour protection worked in and the hull aft cut down to compensate for the added weight; and all were given varying degrees of augmented A/A and subsequently during the war various radar equipments. During the war the light A/A was continually augmented with up to 18 single and twin 20-mm mountings and the removal in some vessels of the 2-pdr weapons. Torpedo tubes and aircraft facilities were generally removed about 1944 and a number of 40-mm (up to 15 in some units) being added.

The class was extensively employed on trade protection duties during the war and a number of losses were suffered.

*Cornwall* and *Dorsetshire* were both sunk by Japanese carrier aircraft off Ceylon, in part a legacy of the Washington Treaty which caused many ships to be designed with inadequate armour protection in order to achieve high speed and adequate firepower. The *Canberra* was torpedoed by Japanese surface forces off Savo Island, yet another instance in part of inadequate armour protection resulting from strict adherence to the Treaty limitations.

*Cumberland* with funnels increased in height and hangar added aft. *Real Photographs*

*Norfolk* early in the war with a Walrus amphibian on the catapult and UP rocket projectors atop B and X turret. *IWM*

*Norfolk* late in the war with gunnery, surface and air warning radar. *IWM*

*Devonshire* as a navigational trainer. *Real Photographs*

## York Class
## *Exeter, York*

Although the 8-in (203-mm) gunned *County* class were built to the limits laid down by the Washington Treaty the Naval Staff considered that a rather smaller cruiser, still armed with 8-in guns, would be required. At the time, 1925, visual spotting was still relied on and the minimum number of guns necessary to achieve effective fire under these conditions was considered to be six. With a requirement that the ships should be capable of steaming at 32 knots, the same as the *County's*, the broad parameters of the new class were already circumscribed. They would carry six 8-in guns in twin turrets; installed power to give 32 knots, would be 80,000 shp; the foc's'le deck would be reduced in length and instead of an upper deck running the whole length of the ship (as in the *County's*) it would end just abaft the bridge; and protection would to some extent be improved because with one turret less, overall length could be reduced resulting in a considerable saving in weight (the *York's* were 50 ft shorter than the *County's*).

The original design showed three funnels as in the *County's*, but as the fore funnel would be sited very close to the bridge it was decided to omit it, and trunk two exhausts into the centre funnel which as a result would be somewhat larger than the after funnel.

An aircraft and catapult were mounted abaft the funnels, plans for mounting a second aircraft and catapult atop B turret being dropped when it was found there was insufficient strength in the turret to support the installation.

Being laid down after the *York*, the *Exeter* incorporated a number of improvements. Both ships were subject to little alteration before their loss, minor changes being made to the light A/A and radar added. *Exeter* was severely damaged at the Battle of the River Plate and was subsequently sunk in the Battle of the Java Sea by the Japanese heavy cruisers *Ashigara* and *Myoko*. *York* was extensively damaged in Suda Bay, Crete, by small Italian explosive motor boats on 26 March, 1941. The vessel was beached and further damaged in German air raids on the island in April and May, and finally abandoned when the British withdrew from the island. The wreck was not removed until after the war when it was salvaged and taken to Bari for scrapping in March 1952.

*Exeter. A & J Pavia*

## Admiral(?) Class

Four 8-in gunned heavy cruisers were projected in 1940 but more urgent war construction led to the abandonment of the scheme. Profiting from lessons learnt with the *County* class, and free of restrictions, these cruisers would have been substantially larger, with much of the extra displacement taken up by increased protection. The main armament would have been as in the *County's* but secondary firepower would have been substantially improved together with a much heavier light A/A battery.

| CLASS | *KENT* | *LONDON* | *DORSETSHIRE* |
|---|---|---|---|
| Displacement | 10,570 | 9,830 (†10,500) | 9,975 (**9,925) |
| **DIMENSIONS** | | | |
| Metric | 192×18.6×6.5 | 193×20×6.5 | 192×20×6.5 |
| Imperial | 630×61×21¼ | 633×66×21½ | 630×66×21½ |
| **MACHINERY** | | | |
| Unit/shafts | GT/4 | GT/4 | GT/4 |
| HP/speed | 80,000/31½ | 80,000/32¼ | 80,000/32¼ |
| Radius/speed | 10,400/14 | 10,400/14 | 10,400/14 |
| Fuel | 3,400 | 3,210 | 3,210 |
| **PROTECTION** | | | |
| Main belt | 38–127 –(1½–5) | 25–140 (1–5½) | 25 (1) |
| Lower deck | 38 –(1½) | 35 (1⅜) | 35 (1⅜) |
| Turrets | 38–50 (1½–2) | 38–50 (1½–2) | 38–50 (1½–2) |
| **ARMAMENT** | | | |
| Guns and torpedo tubes | 8×203/50 (4×2)<br>8×100 –(4×2)<br>8×2pdr –(2×4)<br>8×12.7 (2×4) | 8×203 50–(4×2)<br>8×100 –(8×1, †4×2)<br>16×2pdr (2×8 in† only)<br>8×12.7 (2×4)<br>8×533 (×4) TT | 8×203/50 (4×2)<br>8×100 (4×2)<br>16×2pdr (2×8)<br>8×12.7 (2×4)<br>8×533 (2×4) TT |
| Aircraft/catapults | 3 (*1)/1 | 1 (†3)/1 | 1/1 |
| Complement | 710 | 700(789) | 819 |

| CLASS | *YORK* | *ADMIRAL* |
|---|---|---|
| Displacement | 8,250–8,390 | 18,740 |
| **DIMENSIONS** | | |
| Metric | 175.2×17.3×6.2 | 213.3 |
| Imperial | 575×57×20½ | 700 (?)×NA |
| **MACHINERY** | | |
| Unit shafts | GT/4 | GT/4 |
| HP speed | 80,000/32¼ | 110,000 or 120,000/32¼ |
| Radius speed | 10,000/14 | NA |
| Fuel | 1,900 | NA |
| **PROTECTION** | | |
| Main belt | 76 (3) | 114 (4½) |
| Lower deck | 35 (1⅜) | 76 (2–3) |
| Turrets | 38–50 (1½–2) | NA |
| **ARMAMENT** | | |
| Guns and torpedo tubes | 6×203/50 (2×3)<br>4×100 (4×1)<br>2×2pdr (2×1)<br>6×533 (2×3) TT | 8×203 (4×2)<br>12×100 (6×2) |
| Aircraft/catapults | 1/1 | None |
| Complement | 623–630 | NA |

| NAME | BUILDER | IN SERVICE | FATE | NAME | BUILDER | IN SERVICE | FATE |
|---|---|---|---|---|---|---|---|
| Australia | 23 | 1928 | BU 1955 | Kent | 11 | 1928 | BU 1948 |
| Berwick | 16 | 1928 | BU 1948 | London | 36 | 1929 | BU 1950 |
| Canberra | 23 | 1928 | Lost 9/8/42 | Norfolk | 16 | 1930 | BU 1950 |
| Cornwall | 15 | 1928 | Lost 5/4/42 | Shropshire | 5 | 1929 | BU 1955 |
| Cumberland | 45 | 1928 | BU 1959 | Suffolk | 36 | 1928 | BU 1948 |
| Devonshire | 15 | 1929 | BU 1954 | Sussex | 22 | 1929 | BU 1950 |
| Dorsetshire | 36 | 1930 | Lost 5/4/42 | York | 33 | 1930 | CTL 4–5/41 |
| Exeter | 15 | 1931 | Lost 1/3/42 | | | | |

# UNITED STATES

## Pensacola Class
### *Pensacola, Salt Lake City*

These two heavy cruisers were the first to be built for the US Navy under the Washington Treaty limitations. Work on the design of these vessels did not start until well after contemporary heavy cruisers such as the Japanese *Myoko*, Italian *Trento*, French *Duquesne* and British *Kent* and so the American design was able to profit to some extent from some of the pioneering work carried out on these contemporary designs. The French and Italiams both vied with each other to concentrate on high speed at the sacrifice of protection. The Japanese endeavoured to gain the best of both worlds, concentrating on both speed and protection, but also obtaining heavy firepower, but at the expense of breaking the Treaty limitations, a fact which they were fairly successful at covering up and avoiding discussion on their designs. The British, following the letter of the Treaty to the limit, could not match up to other contemporary designs, being slower, and underarmed compared to those units. They were, however, well built with reasonable protection and were certainly seaworthy ships.

Being designed for Pacific operations, with a view to possible conflict with the Japanese Navy, the design of American heavy cruisers was obviously influenced by developments in the Far East.

The *Pensacola* class were therefore more akin to the Japanese vessels than to their European counterparts. Heavy firepower was essential to match Japanese vessels and the ten-gun arrangement in four mountings of two triple and two twin turrets was adopted, as opposed to the Japanese system of five twin turrets. This was more sensible for while achieving the same broadside, the problems of mounting a third turret forward with limited fore and aft arcs of fire was overcome, not to mention the strain placed on a relatively short section of the hull should all three forward turrets being engaged at the same time.

As in all the cruisers built during the Treaty period, weight considerations were of paramount importance. The Americans were able to keep within the displacement limits by adopting every conceivable weight saving expedient. With only four instead of five turrets they were considerably shorter than their Japanese counterparts (in itself a considerable factor in weight saving) and protection was not up to the same scale as in the Japanese ships (also a weight saving factor). Both classes were flush-decked vessels. The installed power was considerably below that of the Japanese ships (107,000 shp compared to 130,000 shp).

During a subsequent refit the torpedo tubes were removed and the weight saved used to mount extra light A/A, which was to prove a wise decision in the light of war experience, especially as the Americans did not, unlike the Japanese, develop a long-range torpedo.

Various alterations were effected during the war, the light A/A being considerably augmented with six quadruple 40-mm mounts and seventeen single 20-mm, gunnery and warning radar, HA and LA/DCTs and the tripod mainmast being replaced by a light pole mast.

Both cruisers survived the war and were expended during the atom bomb tests at Bikini in 1946.

*Salt Lake City. Real Photographs*

## Northampton Class
### *Augusta, Chester, Chicago, Houston, Louisville, Northampton*

This class was developed from the previous *Pensacola*, and incorporated a number of improvements. The most important of these concerned the weatherly design. It had been found that the low freeboard of the *Pensacola* resulted in the vessels shipping water in heavy weather. This was remedied in the *Northampton's* by giving them an extra deck on the foc's'le which extended aft to the tripod foremast. In the *Augusta, Chicago* and *Houston* this was extended further aft to the catapult amidships to provide extra accommodation for their intended deployment as flagships. In part to compensate for this extra weight it was decided to accept a reduction in firepower of one gun, and to carry nine guns in three triple mounts, thereby saving a considerable amount of weight by completely omitting one turret.

The lack of a hangar for the aircraft on the *Pensacola* was deemed to be a disadvantage (they were stowed in the open on the catapults and on the deck abaft them) and the *Northamptons* carried their four aircraft in a hangar abreast the after funnel.

In other respects the *Pensacola's* and *Northampton's* were very similar and both classes underwent similar updating during the war. The A/A on the *Northamptons* was improved by the addition of four quadruple 40-mm and about 27 single 20-mm as well as the statutory radar.

Compared to the *Pensacola* class the *Northampton's* were noted for rolling, a feature subsequently cured when deeper bilge keels were fitted. Even so the ships were not so comfortable

*Louisville. Real Photographs*

but had a much better stability factor.

Three of the class were lost during the war, the *Chicago* being sunk by Japanese naval aircraft off Rennell Island, the *Houston* by the cruisers *Mikuma* and *Mogami* in the Sunda Straits and the *Northampton* torpedoed by the destroyer *Oyashio* off Lunga Point during the long drawn out battles around Guadalcanal in the autumn and winter of 1942.

*Chester. Real Photographs*

## Portland Class
## *Indianapolis, Portland*

This design was modified from the *Northampton* to incorporate a higher bridge and shorter foremast. Protection was to some extent improved and although the main belt was reduced in length to extend only over the machinery spaces it was made thicker. The weight saved by this stratagem was used to increase the protection on the armoured decks (the lower armoured deck was increased from one to two inches in thickness) and turrets (by about ¾ inch).

War modifications followed the same lines as the previous class. The *Indianapolis* was sunk north of Leyte by the Japanese submarine *I58*.

*Portland. Real Photographs*

Pre-war view of *Minneapolis*. *Marius Bar*

## New Orleans Class
### *Astoria, Minneapolis, New Orleans, Quincy, San Francisco, Tuscaloosa, Vincennes*

This was the last of the Treaty type heavy cruisers to be built for the USN and in spite of those restrictions were exceedingly powerful vessels. Considerable improvements were worked into the design. The machinery layout was re-designed which resulted in the funnels being sited closer together. As a consequence the aircraft and their handling facilities were re-sited abaft the after funnel and the hangar combined with the after superstructure. This enabled the foc's'le deck to be extended right aft to abreast the after funnel. Freeboard was slightly reduced to keep displacement within the required limits but this did not adversely effect the seaworthiness of the cruisers.

The A/A was improved and the ship given increased coverage by siting the leading guns farther forward abreast the bridge.

Protection was also improved, the main belt being extended forward (but not aft) to enclose A barbette; the armour of the decks, turrets and CT was also increased in thickness.

As with other cruisers, war modifications improved A/A capability, four quadruple 1.1-inch mounts being added early in the war, to be subsequently replaced by single 20-mm mounts (19 in all) and four quadruple 40-mm as well as the usual radar.

The *Astoria, Quincy* and *Vincennes* were all sunk by Japanese cruisers off Savo island in August 1942.

*Minneapolis* equipped with gunnery and warning radar. *Real Photographs*

## *Wichita*

This cruiser had originally been planned as the eighth unit of the *New Orleans* class. The design was re-cast on the lines of the *Brooklyn* class light cruisers, and the cruiser resembled a heavy version of the *Brooklyn's* mounting 8-in (203-mm) guns in three triple turrets and a re-arranged secondary 5-in (127-mm) battery, with four of the guns in turrets, three grouped forward around the bridge and one aft, and four beam open mountings abaft the after funnel. The aircraft facilities were also resited aft on the quarterdeck.

Four quad and two twin 40-mm were added during the war together with 20 single 20-mm mounts and radar.

## Baltimore Class

### *Albany (ii)*, Baltimore†, Boston†, Bremerton†, Bridgeport*, Cambridge*, Canberra (ex-Pittsburg)†, Chicago (ii), Columbus, Fall River, Helena (ii) (ex-Des Moines), Kansas City*, Los Angeles, Macon, Norfolk, Northampton (ii)*, Oregon City*, Pittsburg (ii) (ex-Albany), Quincy (ii) (ex-Saint Paul), Rochester (ii)*, Saint Paul (ii) (ex-Rochester), Scranton, Toledo, Tulsa**

The first four vessels in this class were ordered in 1940 under the Two-ocean Programme designed to substantially increase the size of the US Navy with a massive programme of new construction.

The design was closely based on the previous *Wichita* but adopted the arrangement of the *Cleveland* class, carrying 8-inch (203-mm) guns and with a slight increase in size of some 65 ft in length and 4 ft in beam which enabled the ships to mount a heavier A/A battery than the *Cleveland* class.

They were well armed, powerful cruisers with a wide radius of action. In contrast to the previous classes which subsequently

*Helena* in May 1946. *Marius Bar*

*Los Angeles* a few years after the end of the war. Note that catapults on the quarter deck have been removed and a Sikorsky helicopter sits on the deck. *Real Photographs*

had their side scuttles plated over, these vessels were designed with air conditioning and lacked scuttles from the outset. Although the main belt did not extend to cover the bases of the 8-in turrets it was increased in thickness and the ships were considered to have more than adequate protection.

Although a second four cruisers were ordered soon after the first batch, priority at the time was given to other warship types, principally destroyers and destroyer escorts and there was some delay in the completion of these units. Ten more were ordered in 1942 but only six had been completed by the end of the war and four were subsequently cancelled. Of those six three were completed to a modified design (*Albany, Oregon City, Rochester*) with re-designed superstructure and a single large funnel to improve the A/A arcs of fire. In other respects the two groups were identical.

Work on the fourth ship, *Northampton*, was suspended after the war, and she was subsequently completed to a new design as a command ship with extensive communications facilities retaining only the basic hull design and machinery of the earlier vessels.

*Boston, Canberra, Columbus* and *Albany* were converted to guided missile cruisers during the 1950s.

*Rochester*. Note the different bridge structure and single large funnel resulting in improved A/A arcs of fire. *Real Photographs*

## Des Moines Class
### *Dallas (i), Dallas (ii), Des Moines, Newport News, Salem, CA141–CA143, CA149, CA151–CA153*

This was the last class of heavy cruiser to be designed for the US Navy during the war, but only three units were eventually completed.

The design was an enlarged version of the *Oregon City* group of the *Baltimore* class. Length was increased by some 40 ft but the major part of the increase in displacement (altogether about 3,250 tons) was accounted for by increased protection and new power loading gear in the 8-in (203-mm) gun turrets together with cased charges which considerably improved the rate of fire (10-rpm as against 2½-rpm in the older 8-in cruisers).

The A/A armament was also improved. The layout remained as in the previous classes, having been well proven through war experience, but the 40-mm were replaced by a new model 3-in (76-mm) A/A gun, six twin mountings being carried. Two extra HA/LA DCTs were carried and together with radar fitted directors gave these cruisers a formidable controlled A/A firepower capability.

The main belt was extended fore and aft to cover the barbettes, increased in thickness and of greater depth.

These cruisers were the ultimate in heavy cruiser design achieving those qualities most essential in warship design. Unfortunately by the time they were completed they were already becoming outdated by advancing air and missile technology.

## Alaska Class
### *Alaska, Guam, Hawaii, Phillippines, Puerto Rico, Samoa*

The six ships of this class, often referred to as battlecruisers but officially designated by the US Navy as large cruisers, were ordered in 1943.

The design was conceived in reply to the *Chichibu* class which it was believed the Japanese were building and which it was believed were an improved type of German pocket-battleship. This was yet another instance of a class of warships being built in reply to intelligence surveys based on unfounded reports.

The design was loosely based on the *Baltimore* class but with improved protection (although certainly not on the scale of a battlecruiser) and a completely new 12-in (305-mm) gun instead of the 8-in (203-mm), nine of which were mounted in triple turrets.

They were flush decked vessels with a high speed enabling them to act in concert with the fast carrier task forces or with other fast cruisers and they proved to be excellent sea-boats but did not prove to be economical steamers. Aircraft stowage and handling facilities reverted to the midships disposition with this class.

The last three units were cancelled when it was discovered that the reports of the *Chichibu* class were based on false and incorrect information, the decision to cancel being strengthened by the severe shortage of steel being experienced in 1943.

Work on the *Hawaii* was suspended after the war and discussions continued concerning whether she should be completed as a tactical command ship or a guided missile cruiser. It was eventually decided to scrap the 82% completed vessel.

*Des Moines. Real Photographs*

*Newport News. Real Photographs*

| CLASS | *PENSACOLA* | *NORTHAMPTON* | *PORTLAND* | *NEW ORLEANS* |
|---|---|---|---|---|
| Displacement | 9,100 | 9,050 | 9,800–9,950 | 9,375–9,975 |
| **DIMENSIONS** | | | | |
| Metric | 178.5×19.8×6.7 | 183×20×5 | 186×20×5.1 | 179.2×18.8×7.6 |
| Imperial | 585¾×65¼×22 | 600¼×66×16½ | 610¼×66×17 | 588¼×61¾×25 |
| **MACHINERY** | | | | |
| Unit/shafts | GT/4 | GT/4 | GT/4 | GT/4 |
| HP/speed | 107,000/32½ | 107,000/32½ | 107,000/32¾ | 107,000/32¾ |
| Radius/speed | | | | |
| Fuel | 2,895–3,052 | 3,064 | 2,125–2,775 | 2,178–2,270 |
| **PROTECTION** | | | | |
| Main belt | 76 (3) | 76 (3) | 76–100 (3–4) | 38–127 (1½–5) |
| Main deck | 50 (2) | 50 (2) | 50 (2) | 76–3 (3) |
| Lower deck | 25 (1) | 25 (1) | 50 (2) | 13–50 (½–2) |
| Turrets | 38 (1½) | 38–57 (1½–2¼) | 38–76 (1½–3) | 76–127 (3–5) |
| Conning tower | 203 (8) | 203 (8) | 203 (8) | 203 (8) |
| **ARMAMENT** | | | | |
| Guns and torpedo tubes | 10×203/55 (2×3+2×2)<br>8×127/25 (8×1)<br>2×3pdr (2×1)<br>8×12.7 (8×1) | 9×203/55 (3×3)<br>8×127/25 (8×1)<br>2×3pdr (2×1)<br>8×12.7 (8×1) | 9×203/55 (3×3)<br>8×127/25 (8×1)<br>2×3pdr (2×1)<br>8×12.7 (8×1) | 9×203/55 (3×3)<br>8×127/25 (8×1)<br>2×3pdr (2×1)<br>8×12.7 (8×1) |
| Aircraft/catapults | 4/2 | 4/2 | 4/2 | 4/2 |
| Complement | 653 | 621 | 848 | 1,200 |

| CLASS | *WICHITA* | *BALTIMORE* | *ALASKA* | *DES MOINES* |
|---|---|---|---|---|
| Displacement | 9,324 | 13,600 (*13,260) | 27,500 | 17,000 |
| **DIMENSIONS** | | | | |
| Metric | 187×18.8×7.6 | 205.7 (†205.2)×21.5×7.9 | 246.4×27.6×9.8 | 218.3×23.3×7.9 |
| Imperial | 614×61¾×25 | 675 (†73½)×70¾×26 | 808½×90¾×32¼ | 716½×76½×26 |
| **MACHINERY** | | | | |
| Unit/shafts | GT/4 | GT/4 | GT/4 | GT/4 |
| HP/speed | 100,000/32½ | 120,000/33 (*32½) | 150,000/33 | 120,000/33 |
| Radius/speed | | | | |
| Fuel | 2,170 | 2,590–2,735 | 3,710 | 2,600 |
| **PROTECTION** | | | | |
| Main belt | 38–127 (1½–5) | 152 (6) | 127–228 (5–9 | 152–203 (6–8) |
| Main deck | 76 (3) | 76 (3) | 82–108 (3¼–4¼) | 76 (3) |
| Lower deck | 50 (2) | 50 (2) | 50 (2) | 50 (2) |
| Turrets | 76–152 (3–6) | 76–152 (3–6) | 127–324 (5–12¾) | 152 (6) |
| Conning tower | 203 (8) | 203 (8) | 228 (9) | 203 (8) |
| **ARMAMENT** | | | | |
| Guns and torpedo tubes | 9×203/55 (3×3)<br>8×127/38 (8×1)<br>2×3pdr (2×1) | 9×203/55 (3×3)<br>12×127/38 (6×2)<br>48×40 (11×4+2×2, *12×4)<br>22–28×20 (singles) | 9×304/50 (3×3)<br>12×127/38 (6×2)<br>56×40 (14×4)<br>23×20 (34×1) | 9×203/55 (3×3)<br>12×127/38 (6×2)<br>24×76/50 (12×2)<br>12×20 (6×2) |
| Aircraft/catapults | 4/2 | 4/2 | 4/2 | None |
| Complement | 1,200 | 1,700 (*1,969) | 2,251 | 1,799 |

| NAME | BUILDER | IN SERVICE | FATE | NAME | BUILDER | IN SERVICE | FATE |
|---|---|---|---|---|---|---|---|
| Alaska | 31 | 1944 | BU 7/61 | Hawaii | 31 | — | Suspended, BU 1960 |
| Albany | 7 | 1946 | | Helena | 7 | 1945 | Str 1974 |
| Astoria | 37 | 1934 | Lost 8/8/42 | Houston | 29 | 1930 | Lost 1/3/42 |
| Augusta | 29 | 1931 | BU 1960 | Indianapolis | 31 | 1932 | Lost 29/7/45 |
| Baltimore | 7 | 1943 | Str 1971 | Kansas City | 7 | — | Canc 8/45 |
| Boston | 7 | 1943 | Str ? | Los Angeles | 35 | 1945 | Str 1974 |
| Bremerton | 31 | 1945 | Str 1973 | Louisville | 37 | 1931 | BU |
| Bridgeport | 7 | — | Canc 8/45 | Macon | 31 | 1945 | Str 1969–70 |
| Cambridge | 7 | — | Canc 8/45 | Minneapolis | 35 | 1934 | BU 1959 |
| Canberra | 7 | 1943 | | New Orleans | 30 | 1934 | BU 1959–60 |
| Chester | 31 | 1930 | BU 1960 | Newport News | 29 | 1949 | |
| Chicago i | 25 | 1931 | Lost 30/1/43 | Norfolk | 35 | — | Canc 8/45 |
| Chicago ii | 35 | 1945 | | Northampton i | 7 | 1930 | Lost 1/12/42 |
| Columbus | 7 | 1945 | BU 1976 | Northampton ii | 7 | 1953 | |
| Dallas i | 29 | — | Canc 3/45 | Oregon City | 7 | 1946 | Str |
| Dallas ii | 7 | — | Canc 6/45 | Pensacola | 31 | 1930 | Sc 10/11/48 |
| Des Moines | 7 | 1948 | | Philippines | 31 | — | Canc 6/43 |
| Fall River | 31 | 1945 | Str 1971 | Pittsburg | 7 | 1944 | Str 1971 |
| Guam | 31 | 1944 | BU 8/61 | Portland | 7 | 1933 | BU 1960 |

| NAME | BUILDER | IN SERVICE | FATE | NAME | BUILDER | IN SERVICE | FATE |
|---|---|---|---|---|---|---|---|
| Puerto Rico | 31 | — | Canc 6/43 | Scranton | 35 | — | Canc 8/45 |
| Quincy i | 7 | 1936 | Lost 8/8/42 | Toledo | 31 | 1946 | Str 1974 |
| Quincy ii | 7 | 1943 | Str 1971 | Tulsa | 7 | — | Canc 8/45 |
| Rochester | 7 | 1946 | Str | Tuscaloosa | 31 | 1934 | BU |
| Saint Paul | 7 | 1945 | | Vincennes | 7 | 1937 | Lost 8/8/42 |
| Salem | 7 | 1949 | | Wichita | 35 | 1939 | BU 1959–60 |
| Salt Lake City | 31 | 1929 | Expended 7/46 | CA141–143 | 7 | — | Canc 8/45 |
| Samoa | 31 | — | Canc 6/43 | CA 149 | 29 | — | Canc 8/45 |
| San Francisco | 25 | 1934 | BU 1960 | CA 151–153 | 29 | — | Canc 3/45 |

# LIGHT CRUISERS

# FRANCE

## Duguay Trouin Class
*Duguay Trouin, Lamotte Picquet, Primauguet*

The first post World War I programme of construction undertaken by the French Navy provided for the construction of three light cruisers under the 1922 Programme. The estimates were passed in April of that year and work began immediately on preparing plans for the new cruisers. They were designed as high speed cruisers relying on their speed for protection, very little armour being provided. Careful attention was paid to the hull design and propulsion system to enable the ships to maintain a high speed even in adverse weather conditions. In this respect the design was a success and the vessels proved most satisfactory in service, being seaworthy and capable of easily sustaining 30 knots with only half the designed power of 100,000 shp. That the general design of the hull and machinery was excellent was more than proved when in 1949, after 26 years of service the *Duguay Trouin* was still capable of maintaining a speed of 27¾ knots at a full load displacement of 10,900 tons.

For their time they were exceedingly well armed ships carrying eight 6.1-in (155-mm) guns in twin turrets. The 6.1-in gun was chosen in order to simplify and reduce costs in providing ammunition for the French Armed Services — the French Army also deploying a 6.1-in gun.

Very little protection was given to these ships both to contain displacement within the limits set by the Washington Treaty and to enable the required high speed to be achieved. Although only lightly protected (they had no armoured belt and only very light deck armour and splinter proof protection round the turrets) they were provided with 16 watertight bulkheads while abreast the machinery spaces extra coverage was provided by a double shell.

Like most ships designed between the wars they could be said to lack adequate A/A armament, although in fairness it must be noted that the threat of attack from the air had not really become manifest at the time when they were designed. This was to some extent rectified during World War II when the light A/A was augmented, the name-ship of the class losing her torpedo tubes in 1943 and having fifteen single 20-mm and three twin 13.2-mm A/A added. By the end of the war she was carrying six single 40-mm and twenty single 20-mm. The *Primauguet* had been fitted with two single 25-mm and four quadruple 13.2-mm A/A.

*Lamotte Picquet* and *Primauguet* were both lost during the war, *Lamotte Picquet* being sunk in the Far East by American carrier aircraft and *Primauguet* being sunk at Casablanca by the gunfire of American ships during the North African landings. *Duguay Trouin* was disarmed at Alexandria in June 1940, but was subsequently re-fitted and re-armed in 1943 joining Allied naval forces.

*Primauguet* in 1937. *Marius Bar*

*Lamotte Picquet* in January 1930. *Marius Bar*

*Jeanne d'Arc* in March 1932. *Marius Bar*

## *Jeanne d'Arc*

The *Jeanne d'Arc* was designed primarily as a training cruiser for midshipmen and was therefore only lightly armed and had minimal protection.

The main armament was the same as that mounted in the *Duguay Trouin* cruisers. Being designed for a training role she was provided with extensive accommodation.

The *Jeanne d'Arc* was in the French West Indies in June 1940 and following the French surrender was disarmed and immobilised there. She was re-armed in 1943, the torpedo tubes being removed and light A/A improved by the addition of six 40-mm and twenty 20-mm, all in single mounts.

*Jeanne d'Arc* in 1937. *Wright & Logan*

## *Emile Bertin*

When the Italians began designing their light cruisers of the *Condottieri* class the French had no immediate counter. The French *contre-torpilleurs* of the *Malin* and *Maillé Brézé* classes on paper were considered to be slightly inferior to the performance claimed for the Italian cruisers (this did not in fact prove to be the case). To support their destroyers the French therefore designed a new light cruiser, the *Emile Bertin* which was ordered under the 1930 Programme. It was planned that the *Emile Bertin* should be capable of performing a dual function as flagship for the destroyer squadrons and as a minelayer. In the event the light cruiser was never used in the minelaying role.

Being designed as a counter to the Italian cruisers she was given a powerful armament and was the trials ship for the new triple 6-in (152-mm) turret. Three of the new turrets were mounted in A, B and Y positions. For her intended minelaying role she was provided with a heavy A/A armament for self-defence, as she would be operating in enemy waters as a lone unit.

For minelaying operations high transit speed is of vital importance. The French had already shown that they could achieve excellent results with their machinery and like other French ships designed between the wars the *Emile Bertin* more than justified the planners expectations. Designed speed and shaft horsepower was easily exceeded on trials over an eight hour period an average speed of 36.73 knots being recorded at 108,026 shp, the maximum speed being 39.66 knots at 137,908 shp.

To achieve such speeds displacement was kept to a minimum and very little protection was provided. Unfortunately weight had been too restricted and it was found in service that broadside salvoes strained the hull. This was to some extent rectified in 1939 when the ship was under refit and strengthening added.

She was immobilised in the French West Indies in 1940 and was refitted in America during 1943 when radar was added and the A/A altered to eight 3.5-in (90-mm) (3×2, 2×1), 16×40-mm in quad mountings and 20×20-mm. The torpedo tubes were removed together with the aircraft and their facilities.

*Emile Bertin* in 1936. *Marius Bar*

*Jean de Vienne* in July 1938. Note the large catapult aft and massive DCT atop foremast. *Marius Bar*

## La Galissonnière Class

### *La Galissonnière, Georges Leygues, Gloire, Jean de Vienne, Marseillaise, Montcalm*

The success of the *Emile Bertin* design built as a prototype in reply to the Italian *Condottieri* class led to the French designing one of the finest cruiser classes ever to have been built. This class retained the excellent features of previous designs — high speed, well disposed main and secondary armament— and also achieved high standard of protection. The excellent sea-going characteristics of previous classes were also retained.

Two cruisers were authorised in 1932 and were designed under the limitations laid down at the 1932 Geneva Conference, subsequently confirmed by the London Naval Treaty of 1936. A further four cruisers of this class were ordered under the 1933 Programme.

The armament layout was the same as in the *Emile Bertin* but with greatly improved protection the speed fell by 5 knots. They were still, however, very fast ships. Realising that to provide increased protection would mean sacrificing speed and power the French designed the ships for a speed of 31 knots at a rating of 84,000 shp. They anticipated that the cruisers, in common with previous classes, might exceed these figures and reach a speed of about 32 knots on a rating of 97,000 shp. On trials, however, over 100,000 shp was achieved with maximum speeds of 35–36 knots being recorded.

*Georges Leygues* in 1940. *Marius Bar*

During 1941 *Gloire*, *La Galissonnière*, *Georges Leygues* and *Jean de Vienne* were fitted with an extra 37-mm, two single 25-mm and two twin 13.2-mm A/A.

Three of the class were scuttled in Toulon in 1942. Two were subsequently raised, but were finally sunk in an air raid. *Gloire, Montcalm* and *Georges Leygues* were refitted in America during 1943 when the non-standard (compared with other Allied ships) A/A was removed and six quad 40-mm and twenty single 20-mm fitted and radar added. To compensate for added topweight the aircraft and catapult were removed. They underwent a further refit in 1945 when a new radar mast was added abaft the forward tripod mast.

*Montcalm* in 1945 showing changes effected during the refit in the USA. Courtesy of *Musée de la Marine*

## De Grasse Class
### *Chateaurenault, De Grasse, Guichen*

These three cruisers, ordered under the 1937 and 1938 estimates, were designed as improved units of *La Galissonnière* type.

Armament was to be the same as in *La Galissonnière*, but protection was to have been improved. The installed machinery was to have been much more powerful with horsepower increased from the designed 84,000 of *La Galissonnière* to 110,000 shp.

In appearances the ships would have differed considerably. The tripod foremast would have been replaced by a composite bridge structure aft of which would have been a single funnel. The catapult were to be resited aft of the funnel and two would have been carried, one on either beam. Secondary armament would have been concentrated about the after mast.

The *De Grasse* was laid down in November 1938 and all three cruisers were due to be completed in 1941. The outbreak of war caused a severe delay in the construction and two of the cruisers were never laid down. Work on *De Grasse* ceased and she was not eventually launched until 1946. Work re-commenced in 1951 and she was eventually completed as an A/A cruiser.

| CLASS | *DUGUAY TROUIN* | *JEANNE D'ARC* | *EMILE BERTIN* |
|---|---|---|---|
| Displacement | 7,249 | 6,496 | 5,886 |
| **DIMENSIONS** | | | |
| Metric | 181.6×17.2×6.3 | 170×17.7×6.4 | 177×16×6.6 |
| Imperial | $595\frac{3}{4}$×$56\frac{1}{2}$×$20\frac{3}{4}$ | $557\frac{3}{4}$×58×21 | $580\frac{3}{4}$×$52\frac{1}{2}$×$21\frac{3}{4}$ |
| **MACHINERY** | | | |
| Unit/shafts | GT/4 | GT/2 | GT/4 |
| HP/speed | 100,000/33 | 32,500/25 | 102,000/34 |
| Radius/speed | 4,500/15 | 5,200/11 | 3,600/15 |
| Fuel | 1,500 | 1,400 | 1,360 |
| **PROTECTION** | | | |
| Belt | None | None | None |
| Deck | 20 ($\frac{3}{4}$) | NA | 20 ($\frac{3}{4}$) |
| Turrets | 30 ($1\frac{1}{8}$) | None | None |
| Conning tower | 30 ($1\frac{1}{8}$) | 30 ($1\frac{1}{8}$) | 20–30 ($\frac{3}{4}$–$1\frac{1}{8}$) |

| CLASS | *DUGUAM TROUIN* | *JEANNE D'ARC* | *EMILE BERTIN* |
|---|---|---|---|
| **ARMAMENT** | | | |
| Guns and torpedo tubes | 8×155/55 (4×2) | 8×155/55 (4×2) | 9×152/50 (3×3) |
| | 4×75/60 (4×1) | 4×75/60 (4×1) | 4×90 (1×2+2×1) |
| | 12×550 (4×3) TT | 4×37 (2×2) | 8×37 (4×2) |
| | | 12×13.2 | 8×13.2 (4×2) |
| | | 2×550 (2×1) TT | 6×550 (2×3) TT |
| Aircraft/catapults | 2/1 | 2/None | 2/1 |
| Complement | 578 | 460 (+156 trainees) | 711 |

| | *LA GALISSONNIÈRE* | *DE GRASSE* |
|---|---|---|
| Displacement | 7,600 | 8,000 |
| **DIMENSIONS** | | |
| Metric | 179.5×17.5×5.3 | 176.3×18×NA |
| Imperial | $589\times57\frac{1}{4}\times17\frac{1}{2}$ | $578\frac{1}{2}\times59\times$NA |
| **MACHINERY** | | |
| Unit/shafts | GT/2 | GT/2 |
| HP/speed | 84,000/31 | 110,000/35 |
| Radius/speed | 6,800/14 | NA |
| Fuel | 1,569 | NA |
| **PROTECTION** | | |
| Belt | 105(4) | NA |
| Deck | $38(1\frac{1}{2})$ | NA |
| Turrets | 50–100(2–4) | NA |
| Conning tower | $50–95(2–3\frac{1}{2})$ | NA |
| **ARMAMENT** | | |
| Guns and torpedo tubes | 9×152/50(3×3) | 9×152/50 (3×3) |
| | 8×90/50(4×2) | 6×90 (3×2) |
| | 8×37(4×2) | 5×25 (5×1) |
| | 12×13.2 | 8×13.2 (1×4+2×2) |
| | 4×550(2×2) TT | 6×550 (2×3) TT |
| Aircraft/catapults | 4/1 | 3–4/2 |
| Complement | 540 | 580 |

| NAME | BUILDER | IN SERVICE | FATE | NAME | BUILDER | IN SERVICE | FATE |
|---|---|---|---|---|---|---|---|
| Chateaurenault | 19 | — | Canc | Guichen | 18 | — | Canc |
| Duguay Trouin | 9 | 1926 | BU 1952 | Jean de Vienne | 24 | 1937 | Sc 27/11/42, Sz It *FR11* (qv) |
| Emile Bertin | 4 | 1934 | BU 1959 | | | | |
| La Galissonnière | 9 | 1935 | Sc 27/11/42, Sz It *FR12* (qv) | Jeanne d'Arc | 4 | 1931 | BU 1966 |
| | | | | Lamotte Picquet | 24 | 1926 | Lost 12/1/45 |
| Georges Leygues | 4 | 1937 | BU 1959–60 | Marseillaise | 3 | 1937 | Sc 27/11/42 |
| Gloire | 18 | 1937 | BU1958 | Montcalm | 19 | 1937 | BU |
| De Grasse | 24 | 1956 | Str 1973 | Primauguet | 9 | 1926 | Lost 8/11/42 |

# THE NETHERLANDS

## Java Class
### *Celebes, Java, Sumatra**

The design for these cruisers was drawn up in 1916 and although classed as light cruisers, by virtue of their armament, they were much larger than contemporary British and German light cruisers. The decision to build larger cruisers than the British and Germans was influenced by the requirement that the vessels should be capable of firing a broadside of seven guns with a fore and aft fire of four to five guns. So although they were much larger than contemporary light cruisers their firepower was greatly increased.

Completion of *Java* and *Sumatra* was delayed and requirements altered considerably following the end of the war. Further the Washington Treaty placed limits on cruiser design and in view of these factors it was decided to cancel the order for the *Celebes*, which had not in fact been laid down at that time.

The design of the *Java* and *Sumatra* was rendered obsolete. Attempts were made to update the cruisers and they were provided with aircraft handling facilities, carrying two seaplanes, but no flying off capabilities were provided.

The ships were further refitted in 1934–5 when a substantial tubular mast carrying a gunnery director replaced the pole foremast, while the mainmast was resited farther forward and shortened. During this refit the four old 3-in (76-mm) A/A were removed and between six and eight 40-mm added aft, and heavy machine guns mounted in the upper bridge wings which were extended over the top of the samson posts which carried the derricks for handling the aircraft.

The *Java* was in the Far East when war broke out, and remained there to defend the Dutch possessions. She was eventually sunk by the Japanese cruisers *Haguro* and *Nachi* off Bawean Island during the Battle of the Java Sea.

The *Sumatra* escaped to join the Allied Forces but owing to her age and outdated equipment it was found impossible to maintain the ship and she was eventually expended as a breakwater for the Normandy landings in 1944.

*Java* in May 1937. *Wright & Logan*

*Java* in May 1937. *Wright & Logan*

*De Ruyter. Real Photographs*

## *De Ruyter*

The design of this cruiser was a smaller, re-worked version of the cancelled *Celebes* of the *Java* class. It was proposed to limit the tonnage to 5,250 tons and mount only six 5.9-in (150-mm) instead of the ten in the previous class. However, these 5.9-in were to be mounted in a new twin turret, one sited in A position and two in X and Y positions.

There was considerable argument over the scale and disposition of the main armament, many people considering that to be effective the cruiser should carry four twin 5.9-in turrets instead of three. However it was found that the tonnage restrictions would be completely impractical for mounting even three twin turrets and so an increase in size was permitted which allowed the designers to improve the hull lines, increase the overall length (she was some 50-ft longer than the *Java*) and install more powerful machinery than originally planned, although still not as powerful that in the *Java*. The increase in length also allowed the designers to reach a compromise and mount a single 5.9-in gun in B position instead of the twin mount so many considered necessary. The extra gun certainly improved the ahead arcs of fire. There was no secondary armament although she did mount a powerful battery of twin 40-mm A/A aft.

To save weight and space it was decided to adopt a two-shaft arrangement for propulsion, although this was not an altogether satisfactory solution for it left the mobility of the ship vulnerable to battle damage.

She was distinguished by a prominent smoke deflector to her funnel. Abaft the funnel was sited the catapult and aircraft stowage facilities. The bridge was similar to that of the German *Admiral Graf Spee*, being a tall tower structure housing the control stations and topped by DCT.

*De Ruyter* was serving in the Far East on the outbreak of war and was sunk in the Battle of the Java Sea.

## Tromp Class
## *Jacob van Heemskerck, Tromp*

These two ships were designed originally in 1931 as flotilla leaders of 2,500 tons. In the knowledge that the Japanese were building much more powerful fleet destroyers the design for these vessels was recast to provide armour protection for vital areas such as machinery spaces, magazines etc. It was still envisaged that the ships would operate in support of the Dutch destroyer squadrons and to this end it was a specific staff requirement that they should be capable of maintaining a high speed with good manoeuvrability characteristics.

*Tromp* was completed just before the war, but the *van Heemskerck* was still under construction when war broke out. Just before the Germans occupied Holland she was towed over to England and completed by Portsmouth dockyard. As no fire control equipment had been fitted, and none of suitable type was available it was decided to rearm the *van Heemskerck* as an A/A cruiser using British equipment. This resulted in the torpedo tube mountings and aircraft being omitted and the foc's'le deck level being extended further aft from the funnel to the mainmast. The 5.9-in (150-mm) guns in A, B and Y positions were replaced by twin 4-in (100-mm) A/A mounts, while two extra midships beam twin 4-in were sited where the aircraft would have been carried. The guns were controlled by a standard British HA/DCTs fore and aft and radar, both air warning and fire control, added.

Both vessels served extensively throughout the war, the *Tromp* being updated with radar, the aircraft removed and A/A capability improved by the addition of four single 3-in (76-mm) mounts. The original twin 40-mm mounts were replaced by two twin 40-mm Hazemeyer and six single 20-mm replaced the obsolete 12.7-mm. *Van Heemskerck* subsequently had her quadruple 2-pdr mount replaced by two twin 40-mm Hazemeyer mounts together with two extra twin 40-mm mounts added amidships and four twin 20-mm replacing the single 20-mm mounts.

*Tromp* in 1938. *Wright & Logan*

*Tromp.* Note radar aerial on short mast on top of bridge and radar atop rangefinder on bridge. Aft are two 40 mm Hazemeyer mountings. *Real Photographs*

## De Zeven Provincien Class
## *De Zeven Provincien, Eendracht (ex-Kijkduin)*

These two cruisers ordered in 1937–38 were originally designed as enlarged versions of *De Ruyter*, with greater improved firepower and better protection. It was planned that the two cruisers would replace the old *Java* and *Sumatra*.

Initial designs showed the vessels mounting light 5.9-in (150-mm) twin turrets, but this was subsequently altered to ten 5.9-in carried in triple turrets in A and Y positions, and twin turrets in B and X positions. The light A/A was also to be much heavier than previous cruisers, consisting of six twin 40-mm Bofors. In addition the cruisers were to be armed with two triple torpedo tubes and abaft the funnel were two catapult launched aircraft.

Installed power was to be 78,000 shp on two shafts to give the vessels a speed of 32 knots. The protection was generally to have followed that of *De Ruyter* with a broad armoured belt enclosing the barbettes of A and Y guns.

Work on the two cruisers was at a very early stage when Holland was occupied by Germany. The *Kijkduin*, laid down on May 19, 1939, was renamed *Eendracht* and the *De Zeven Provincien* was laid down on September 5, 1939. The Dutch were unable to destroy the assembled material and under German supervision work continued. The Germans had hoped to complete the vessels for their own use and *De Zeven Provincien* was in fact given the German 'Atlantic' type bow (as in the *Scharnhorst, Bismarck* etc.). The Dutch cleverly procastinated to such an extent that *De Zeven Provincien* was not able to be launched until December 1944, and then only for use as a blockship, an event which did not materialise.

Both hulls were still intact at the end of the war and the vessels subsequently completed to a recast design, *De Zeven Provincien* being renamed *De Ruyter*, and *Eendracht* renamed *de Zeven Provincien*.

| CLASS | *JAVA* | *DE RUYTER* | *TROMP* | *DE ZEVEN PROVINCIEN* |
|---|---|---|---|---|
| Displacement | 6,670 | 6,442 | 3,787 | 9,325 |
| **DIMENSIONS** | | | | |
| Metric | 155.2×16×5.4 | 171×15.6×5.8 | 132×12.5×4.5 | 187×17.2×5.6 |
| Imperial | 509½×52½×18 | 561×51¼×19¼ | 433×40¾×15 | 613½×56½×18½ |
| **MACHINERY** | | | | |
| Unit/shafts | T/3 | GT/2 | GT/2 | GT/3 |
| HP/speed | 72,000/31 | 66,000/32 | 56,000/33½ | 78,000/32 |
| Radius/speed | 3,600/15 | 5,000/12 | NA | NA |
| Fuel | 1,200 | 1,000 | 860 | 1,750 |
| **PROTECTION** | | | | |
| Belt | 50–76 (2–3) | 50–76 (2–3) | 18 (⅝) | 76–100 (3–4) |
| Deck | 25–50 (1–2) | 32 (1¼) | 25 (1) | NA |
| Turrets | 100 (4) | 50–100 (2–4) | 18 (⅝) | 50–100 (2–4) |
| Conning tower | 127 (5) | NA | 25 (1) | NA |
| **ARMAMENT** | | | | |
| Guns and torpedo tubes | 10×150 (10×1)<br>8(*6)×40 (singles)<br>4×12.7 (4×1)<br>12 mines | 7×150 (3×2+1×1)<br>10×40 (5×2)<br>8×12.7 (4×2) | 6×150 (3×2)<br>8×40 (4×2)<br>4×12.7 (×2)<br>6×533 (2×3) TT | 10×150 (2×3+2×2)<br>14×40 (7×2)<br>8×12.7 (4×2)<br>6×533 (2×3) TT |
| Aircraft/catapults | 2/None | 2/1 | 1/None | 2/2 |
| Complement | 525 | 435 | 309 | 700 |

| NAME | BUILDER | IN SERVICE | FATE |
|---|---|---|---|
| Celebes | — | — | Canc |
| Eendracht | 38 | 1953 | Peru *Almirante Grau* 1973 |
| Jacob Van Heemskerck | 28 | 1940 | |
| Java | 28 | 1925 | Lost 27/2/42 |
| De Ruyter | 48 | 1936 | Lost 27/2/42 |
| Sumatra | 14 | 1925 | Breakwater 9/6/44 |
| Tromp | 28 | 1938 | |
| De Zeven Provincien | 48 | 1953 | Peru *Aguirre* 1976 |

# SOVIET UNION

## *Komintern (ex-Pamyat Merkurya)*

This cruiser, completed during the Russo-Japanese war, was obsolete by the end of World War I. During the intervention in the Russian Revolution, British forces destroyed her machinery in 1919 and the hulk was abandoned in Sevastopol when the White Russian forces withdrew from the Black Sea area in 1920.

The wreck was repaired and re-commissioned into the new Soviet Navy in 1923 as a training ship.

She was active in the Black Sea during World War II and was severely damaged in air raids in July 1942, being finally used as a breakwater in the harbour at Poti.

## *Chervonaya Ukraina (ex-Admiral Nakhimov)*

Laid down as the *Admiral Nakhimov* in 1913 work on this cruiser ceased during the Russian Revolution. Work commenced in 1922 and she was renamed *Chervonaya Ukraina* in December of that year.

Numerous alterations were made to the designs and when completed she carried all but two of her main battery guns at main deck level. There they suffered severe penalties, particularly the four forward guns which were mounted in casemates. These were continually swamped with water in heavy seas and were almost impossible to operate. The guns farther aft, two of which were also in casemates, also suffered, but to a lesser extent.

The machinery was of poor standard, outdated, and not particularly well maintained and although designed for 32 knots, this was never achieved in practice.

She was fitted with two cranes abreast the fore funnel for handling the seaplane carried between the two funnels. This was removed prior to the start of World War II.

During the war the torpedo tubes were removed and the weight saved used to augment the A/A, the six single 76-mm being replaced by twelve 37-mm.

*Chernovaya Ukraina. Real Photographs*

The cruiser was bombed and severely damaged at Sevastopol in November 1941, the hulk sinking in shallow water the following day. A number of guns were landed from the wreck and used by Soviet land forces. The wreck was finally destroyed in an air raid on April 2, 1942.

## *Krasny Krim (ex-Klara Zetkin, ex-Profintern, ex-Svetlana)*

This cruiser, laid down in December 1913, was towed to St. Petersburg in 1916 for completion. Work on the vessel ceased during the Russian Revolution and did not recommence until 1922. A trial cruise, when she was almost complete, was carried out in February 1925 under the name of *Klara Zetkin*, but significant failures to equipment caused the vessel to be laid up for nearly two years while repairs were affected.

She was renamed *Profitern* in 1927 and finally commissioned a year later by which time numerous alterations had been made to the original design. She transferred to the Black Sea in 1929–30 and renamed yet again in 1939 as *Krasny Krim*.

The alterations affected to the initial design considerably improved the ahead fire.

The majority of the main armament was sited low down at main deck level, four of the forward and two of the after guns being sited in casemates. They suffered from poor disposition and the forward casemate guns in particular were almost impossible to work in heavy weather.

The cruiser having been built for service in the Baltic, lacked side armour so that special hull strengthening could be fitted for ice navigation. It is unlikely that any side armour was ever subsequently fitted to the ship.

Machinery, although designed for 32 knots, was decidedly inferior in quality and the best speed achieved by the *Krasny Krim* was 29 knots.

The cruiser was originally equipped with a seaplane, two cranes being carried abreast the fore funnel for handling the aircraft. The aircraft was, however, landed prior to the war.

During the war the torpedo tubes were removed and A/A firepower improved with the addition of ten 37-mm and possibly two 3.9-in (100-mm), although this is not certain.

She served throughout the war in the Black Sea being principally used, as were other large Soviet vessels, in a gunfire support role for ground troops and as a troop transport, especially during the long drawn out siege of Sevastopol.

*Krasy Krym. Authors Collection*

## *Krasny Kavkaz (ex-Admiral Lazarev)*

Like the previous two cruisers, work on this vessel, laid down just before World War I, ceased during the Russian Revolution. When work on the vessel began again in 1924 she was renamed *Krasny Kavkaz*, and like the other two cruisers was completed to a recast design.

She was originally ordered as a sister-ship to the *Chervonaya Ukraina*, but the recast design emerged as a totally different vessel armed with much larger calibre guns mounted on the centre-line fore and aft in the more usual A, B, X, Y, configuration then being adopted for light cruiser armament.

The recasting of the design seriously delayed work and she did not finally commission until 1932. Almost at once she was seriously damaged when in collision with the *Komintern*. During the repairs a new swan-neck bow was fitted reminiscent of the Japanese cruisers. The opportunity was also taken to lengthen the vessel by some 14–15 ft.

As originally completed she carried a catapult and two seaplanes abaft the after funnel with a large crane on the mainmast for handling the aircraft. These, together with two of the torpedo tube mountings were removed about 1939–40 to allow extra A/A to be carried.

The main armament consisted of experimental 7.1-in (180-mm) guns mounted in single turrets. The single 3.9-in (100-mm) guns were replaced during the war by twin 3.9-in.

The cruiser served throughout the war and was severely damaged on a number of occasions. She survived the war and was eventually expended as a target in guided missile trials.

*Krasnji Kavkaz.* P.Vicary

## Kirov Class
### *Kaganovich*, Kalinin*, Kirov, Maksim Gorky*, Molotov*, Voroshilov*

With the success of the 7.1-in (180-mm) mounted experimentally in the *Krasny Kavkaz*, the Soviets authorised a new cruiser class to be designed around this armament. Lacking sufficient technical expertise to design such a vessel the Soviet authorities followed up the approaches they had already made with foreign countries for the design and construction of new warships to build up their Fleet. (*See* Fact File on Battleships page 36). One of the companies approached was the Italian firm of Ansaldo. At the time Italy had under construction the third and fourth cruiser groups of the *Condottieri* type to a design prepared by Umberto Pugliese and the outward appearance of the *Kirov* class resembled very closely that of those Italian cruisers.

With the new cruiser design prepared with Italian technical and construction assistance from Ansaldo the *Kirov* class vessels were laid down between late 1935 and 1939, two each for the Baltic, Black Sea and Pacific Fleets. The first two vessels completed, *Kirov* and *Voroshilov* differed slightly from the remaining vessels.

A dual propulsion system was fitted with diesels being used for economical cruising at 15–17 knots and geared turbines for main propulsion when speed was required (35.94 knots was recorded on trials). The use of diesels considerably extended their radius of action, although by normal standards the actual radius attained (3,000 miles at 14 knots) was very poor and indicates that the cruisers were certainly not economical steamers!

The ships were completed with a catapult between the funnels and carried two aircraft, but these were removed soon after the German invasion of the Soviet Union and extra A/A added.

The *Kirov* and *Voroshilov* were completed with a heavy tripod foremast similar to that in the Italian heavy cruisers, but the rest of the class were completed with a large control and a light tripod mast abaft it as in the Italian *Condottieri* light cruisers.

*Kalinin. Authors Collection*

*Molotov* in 1939. *Real Photographs*

*Murmansk* at Spithead before being handed back to the United States Navy in February 1949. Note the large mattress radar aerials. *P. Vicary*

## Chapayev Class
## *Chapayev, Chkalov, Frunze, Kuibishev, Ordzhonikidze, Zhelezniakov*

Design work on these cruisers began in the late 1930s (about 1937–38) and a total of twelve cruisers were planned, but only six were ever laid down. Again the design was prepared with the assistance of the Italians and the vessels closely resembled in outward appearance Italian cruisers.

Although much larger than the *Kirov* class, the *Chapayev* class carried a much lighter gun, a 5.9-in (150-mm) instead of the 7.1-in (180-mm) of the *Kirov* class. However, the increase in size enabled the ships to carry an extra triple mount, thereby to some extent compensating by increase in the number of broadsides the lack of weight of the broadside. To some extent this was justified for a greater increase in the rate of fire and hence the weight of broadside fired in a given time was bound to tell on an adversary, providing of course that the adversary did not have armour sufficient to protect it against 5.9-in shells. However, there was an added bonus in the choice of the 5.9-in weapon in that it was capable of 50 degree elevation, thus making it suitable for use in case of air attack, a feature that the 7.1-in gun did not have. The 5.9-in gun was also a much more modern and efficient weapon than the 7.1-in. The firepower was further enhanced by the fitting of twin 3.9-in (100-mm) mounts with a dual purpose capability.

Originally, like the *Kirov* class cruisers they were to have carried aircraft and torpedo facilities, but these plans were not implemented.

Of the vessels laid down none were completed until post war owing to grave shortages of steel and the heavy raids carried out on Soviet shipyards, (those in the Black Sea actually falling into German hands), which seriously disrupted work. The *Ordzhonikidze* and an unidentified hull (possibly of the *Chapayev* class) were destroyed on the slip by the Germans.

# FOREIGN CRUISERS

## Ex-American Omaha Class
## *Murmansk (ex-Milwaukee)*

The ex-American cruiser *Milwaukee* (see page 52) was transferred to the Soviet Union in April 1944 along with the *Royal Sovereign* (*see* Fact File on Battleships, page 35) as a temporary measure until agreement could be reached concerning which surrendered Italian warships should be given to the Soviet Union as war reparations. She was returned to America in March 1949.

## Ex-German Hipper Class
## *Tallinn (ex-Petropavlovsk, ex-Lützow)*

Following the Russo-German pact of 1939 a request was made to buy two *Hipper* class cruisers and to build two more in Soviet yards. The Germans continually prevaricated over the request and finally only agreed to transfer one incomplete cruiser, the *Lützow*. The cruiser was towed to Leningrad in 1940 and renamed *Petropavlovsk*. The ship was never completed and was mainly used as a floating battery being renamed *Tallinn* in 1943.

| CLASS | *KOMINTERN* | *CH. UKRAINA* | *KR. KRIM* |
|---|---|---|---|
| Displacement | 6,338 | 6,934 | 6,934 |
| **DIMENSIONS** | | | |
| Metric | 134.2 (pp)×16.6×6.8 | 158.4 (pp)×15.3×6.5 | 154.5 (pp)×15.4×5.6 |
| Imperial | 440¼ (pp)×54½×22¼ | 519¾ (pp)×49¼×21¼ | 487 (pp)×50½×18½ |
| **MACHINERY** | | | |
| Unit/shafts | VTE/2 | GT/2 | GT/2 |
| HP/speed | 19,500/23 | 50,000/29½ | 50,000/29 |
| Radius/speed | 5,300/12 | 3,700/18 | 3,700/18 |
| Fuel | 1,100 | 1,230 | 2,900 |
| **PROTECTION** | | | |
| Belt | None | None | None |
| Deck | 38–70 (1½–2¾) | 25 (1) | 25 (1) |
| Turrets | 76 (3) | 45 (1¾) | 50 (2) |
| Conning tower | 140 (5½) | 76 (3) | 76 (3) |
| **ARMAMENT** | | | |
| Guns and torpedo tubes | 10×130 (10×1)<br>6×75 (6×1)<br>3×76 (3×1)<br>2×47 (2×1) | 15×130 (15×1)<br>6×76 (6×1)<br>12mg<br>12×533 (4×3) TT<br>100 mines | 15×130 (15×1)<br>6×100 (6×1)<br>4×45 (4×1)<br>12×533 (4×3) TT<br>100 mines |
| Aircraft/catapults | None | None | None |
| Complement | 590 | 750 | 684 |

| CLASS | *KR. KAVKAZ* | *KIROV* | *CHAPAYEV* |
|---|---|---|---|
| Displacement | 8,030 | 8,800 (*8,177) | 11,300 |
| **DIMENSIONS** | | | |
| Metric | 166×15.3×6.2 | 191×18 (*17.7)×6.1 (*6.3) | 201 (pp)×19.5×7.1 |
| Imperial | 544½×50¼×20¼ | 626¼×59 (*58)×20 (*20¾) | 659¼ (pp)×64×23¾ |
| **MACHINERY** | | | |
| Unit/shafts | GT/2 | GT/2 | GT/2 |
| HP/speed | 55,000/29 | 113,000 (*129,000)/35 | 130,000/34 |
| Radius/Speed | 3,700/NA | 3,000/18 | 7,000/20 |
| Fuel | 1,600 | 1,280 | 3,500 |
| **PROTECTION** | | | |
| Main belt | None | 75 (3) | NA |
| Main deck | 25–38 (1–1½) | 50 (2) | NA |
| Turrets | 76 (3) | 100 (4) | NA |
| Conning tower | 76 (3) | 75 (3) | NA |
| **ARMAMENT** | | | |
| Guns and torpedo | 4×180 (4×1)<br>10×100 (5×2)<br>4×45 (4×1)<br>8×37 (8×1)<br>6×533 (2×3) TT<br>100 mines | 9×180 (3×3)<br>6×100 (6×1)<br>6×45 (not in *)<br>10×37 (in * only)<br>4×12.7<br>6×533 (2×3) TT, 90 mines | 12×150 (4×3)<br>8×100 (4×2)<br>24×37 (12×2)<br>200 mines |
| Aircraft/catapults | None | 1/1 (not in *) | None |
| Complement | 850 | 734 (*953) | 840 |

| NAME | BUILDER | IN SERVICE | FATE | NAME | BUILDER | IN SERVICE | FATE |
|---|---|---|---|---|---|---|---|
| Chapayev | 32 | 1949 | BU 1961 | Krasny Kavkaz | 40 | 1932 | Expended 6/50 |
| Chervonaya Ukraina | 40 | 1927 | Lost 2/4/42 | Krasny Krim | | 1928 | BU 1958 |
| Chkalov | 32 | 1950 | BU | Kuibishev | 26 | 1950 | BU |
| Frunze | 27 | 1950 | BU 1960s | Maksim Gorky | 32 | 1940 | BU 1958 |
| Kaganovich | 1 | 1944 | BU 1960s | Molotov | 27 | 1941 | BU |
| Kalinin | 1 | 1943 | BU | Ordzhonikidze | 27 | — | BU 1941 |
| Kirov | 32 | 1938 | BU | Voroshilov | 27 | 1940 | BU 1960s |
| Komintern | 40 | 1905 | CTL 16/7/42 | Zhelezniakov | | 1949 | |

# UNITED KINGDOM

## Birmingham Class
## *Adelaide*

The Australian cruiser *Adelaide* was the sole survivor of the *Birmingham* class, the British units all having been scrapped before the start of World War II.

The *Adelaide* (and her sister ships) were designed for trade route protection duties which required a large radius of action and seaworthiness. With this requirement armour was confined to such as was necessary to provide protection for the vessels during surface action. The waterline belt extended the full length of the ship and amidships abreast the machinery spaces this was extended for the full depth of the ships above the waterline. The cruisers lacked any form of armoured transverse bulkhead and had only thin deck armour.

It was proposed to give the *Adelaide* an extensive refit in 1938–39 which would have involved converting the eight coal fired boilers (the other four were oil fired) to oil-burners and trunking the exhausts from the after boiler rooms into a single funnel, removing the third and fourth funnels. During the refit it was proposed that three of the 6-in (152-mm) should be removed while the remainder would be resited on the keel line. Light A/A weapons were to be added (two 4-in (100-mm) amidships, two 2 pdr and associated high angle directors) and to rebuild the bridge.

However, the proposed alterations were reduced in scope and eventually the *Adelaide* emerged from her refit with the forward boiler room closed down (the two boilers were removed together with the fore funnel), and the remaining ten boilers converted to small tube Yarrow oil firing. The main armament remained substantially the same except that the two beam fo'c'sle 6-in guns were removed, and a single 6-in mounted in B position. Two 4-in were added aft together with an extra 4-in on the after superstructure (replacing a 12-pdr weapon). The torpedo tubes were also removed.

Being weakly armoured and lacking adequate A/A protection the cruiser was obsolete for modern warfare but provided valuable protection for convoys during the war. The A/A was marginally improved by the addition of a number of 20 mm A/A.

She was finally sold for scrap in January 1949.

## C Class
## *Cairo*†, *Calcutta*†, *Caledon, Calypso, Capetown*†, *Caradoc, Cardiff (ex-Caprice), Carlisle (ex-Cawnpore)*†, *Ceres, Colombo, Coventry (ex-Corsair)**, *Curacao*†, *Curlew**

These light cruisers formed part of a large group (some were scrapped before the war) which was divided into a number of sub-groups and which varied in numerous details.

The design was based on World War I experience and the vessels lacked certain fundamental features which, by 1939 had become essential to warship design. Principally these concerned the armour and armament connected with aerial warfare. In fairness it must be noted that lack of such essential features in a World War I design could not be levelled against the designers. Aerial warfare in 1914–16 had certainly not reached a stage where it was to have a significant effect on naval strategy and warship design.

*Calypso. Real Photographs*

*Carlisle* in 1918 with aircraft hangar under bridge. *P. Vicary*

*Colombo* in October 1925. *Authors Collection*

The lack of armour protection in these light cruisers arose partly as a consequence of improvement in other design features. The ships were designed with oil-firing boilers which meant that strategically sited coal-bunkers which materially assisted with protection, were no longer available for such purpose in new warships with oil fired boilers. Thus previous light cruisers had only been fitted with internal deck protection. The *C* class light cruisers had, perforce, to be provided with adequate side armour to compensate for this loss and consequently deck armour was to all intents and purposes negligible. The side armour was extended upwards to the upper deck to provide adequate protection against plunging shellfire, but protection against bombs was not a considered necessity at that time.

The *Caledon* was fitted with an aircraft flying-off ramp which was removed in 1918 and replaced by a revolving platform amidships. The ships were refitted and the bridges rebuilt in the 1920s while in 1932 the aircraft equipment was removed from *Caledon*.

The vessels of Group II differed significantly from those of Group I in that the bridge was sited farther aft and the 6-in (152-mm) gun abaft the bridge resited on a shelter deck in front of the bridge, superimposed over 'A' gun.

Group III, although basically similar to Group II differed in that they had a marked sheer up to the fo'c'sle to improve seaworthiness. It was also planned that they should be completed with an aircraft hangar in the bridge, but only the *Carlisle* was completed with the hangar, which was subsequently removed.

Groups II and III underwent extensive refits in 1930s during which *Coventry* and *Curlew* were converted to A/A vessels in a prototype role, the intention being to convert the remainder of the Groups II and III to A/A cruisers. The conversion involved the minimum of structural alterations. All original armament was removed, together with the after superstructure and the bridge modified. For the intended A/A role the two cruisers were equipped with ten 4-in (100-mm) in single mounts — one on the fo'c'sle, one on either beam abreast the forward funnel, two *en echelon* abaft the second funnel, two on the upper deck aft, one on the after shelter deck and two on the quarterdeck. Two multiple 2-pdr mountings were also fitted, but the after mount was subsequently taken off as there was a general shortage of these mounts.

Trials with the two cruisers following this 1935 refit showed the value of the conversion, but only *Curacao* of Group II was similarly converted along the lines of Group III vessels. In

Group III all but *Colombo* underwent a similar, but less extensive, conversion to A/A cruisers in 1938–39. In these vessels all but one of the 6-in guns was replaced by twin 4-in A/A; the second 6-in gun was replaced by a multiple 2-pdr.

Numerous modifications were carried out on all three groups during the war. These included the addition of Air and Surface warning radar and light 20-mm A/A. *Caledon* was converted to an A/A ship in 1942–43 and fitted with a new bridge. She then carried three twin 4-in A/A, two twin 40-mm and six twin 20-mm. Subsequently a further three 40-mm and two 20-mm were added. *Caradoc* remained unaltered until decommissioned in 1944.

*Coventry* landed two of her 4-in in 1940 but two 20-mm and a multiple .5-in (127-mm) were added. *Curacao* and *Ceres* received four 20-mm, and *Cardiff* six 20-mm, *Cardiff* then being used as a gunnery training ship.

Group III vessels were given a total of eight 20-nn in single mounts which were subsequently replaced by twin mounts. *Colombo* was converted to an A/A cruiser in 1942 and armed with three twin 4-in, 14–16 20-mm and two multiple 2-pdr.

*Curlew* modified as an A/A escort. *Real Photographs*

## Cavendish Class
### *Effingham*, Frobisher, Hawkins†, Vindictive (ex-Cavendish)*

These cruisers (together with their sister ship *Vindictive*) were a superior *C* type cruiser designed in 1915–16 in response to an unsubstantiated report that Germany was fitting her armed merchant cruisers with a much heavier gun armament. When the design was being formulated two alternative gun armaments were proposed. One suggested a mixed armament of 9.2-in (234-mm) and 6-in (152-mm), while the other opted for a single calibre of 7.5-in (190-mm). In the end it was decided that the new cruisers should mount a standard armament of 7.5-in. As such they therefore formed an intermediary design stage between the light cruisers and the then defunct armoured cruisers, subsequently supplanted by the heavy cruiser (but which had not appeared at the time these cruisers were designed).

As they were designed to deal with commerce raiders the design considerations of these cruisers called for a high speed (30 knots) and wide radius of action. To render the vessels more independent of overseas bases and restrictions on fuel supplies they were fitted with both coal and oil firing boilers.

Armour protection was on a similar scale to the previous *C* class but certain improvements were incorporated such as increasing the extent of deck armour with extra protection over the boiler and machinery spaces.

When completed the main armament was sited in a similar way to that on the *C* class. In addition the design provided for them to carry a secondary armament of twelve single 12-pdr guns. When completed only *Vindictive* was armed with 12-pdr weapons, six being carried. Six torpedo tubes (four amidships above water and two submerged forward) were also carried.

The ships underwent numerous refits between the wars, all being converted to fully oil-fired vessels. The *Cavendish* was completed in a hurry as she had been selected for conversion to

*Vindictive* as a repair ship. *Real Photographs*

an aircraft carrier carrying up to eight aircraft and renamed *Vindictive*. A variety of 3-in (76-mm) or 4-in (100-mm) A/A guns were fitted in lieu of the 12-pdr weapons. *Vindictive* was subsequently converted to a training ship prior to the war and the *Raleigh* was wrecked in 1922.

Only *Effingham, Frobisher* and *Hawkins* saw war service, the *Effingham* having been extensively modernised just prior to the outbreak of war. *Frobisher* and *Hawkins* were to have been similarly modernised, but the outbreak of war caused this to be cancelled. They were instead given additional A/A armament during the war [multiple 2-pdr (8-in *Hawkins*, 16 in *Frobisher*) and 7–8 20-mm, subsequently increased] as well as radar.

*Effingham* was wrecked in May 1940, but *Frobisher* and *Hawkins* both served throughout the war to be scrapped in 1949 and 1947 respectively.

*Hawkins* in 1934. *A & J Pavia*

*Hawkins. Real Photographs*

*Vindictive* in 1919 completed as an aircraft carrier. *P. Vicary*

*Effingham* – note the single funnel and built up bridge structure. *Real Photographs*

## D Class

### *Danae, Dauntless, Delhi*, Despatch*, Diomede*, Dragon, Dunedin*, Durban**

Like the *Cavendish* class the design of these cruisers was inspired by an unfounded report that Germany was building cruisers superior to the British *C* class. It was at that time (1916) considered that the *C* class had been the ultimate in 6-in (152-mm) cruiser design and that to design a more powerful cruiser, identical in design concept, but carrying more guns to improve firepower, the designers would have to accept a reduction in speed.

The resulting design was the *D* class, three of which were ordered in 1916. The design layout was very similar to the *C* class but length was increased slightly (by some 20-ft) to enable the extra 6-in gun to be mounted. The machinery was very similar to that in the *C* class and with improved propeller efficiency there was very little loss in speed.

Offensive power was further increased by mounting triple instead of twin torpedo tubes, giving the ships a total of 12 tubes.

*Dauntless* and *Dragon* were completed with an aircraft hangar built into the bridge while remaining units, except *Danae*, had flying off platforms aft.

Between the wars the ships had their 3-in (76-mm) A/A replaced by 4-in (100-mm) while early in World War II radar was added and a number of 20-mm A/A. Various other armament changes were affected.

The *Delhi* was re-armed in America as an A/A cruiser during 1941–42. A new bridge was built and new masts fitted and American designed 5-in (127-mm) DP guns replaced the 6-in (152-mm) guns. Light A/A was composed of 2-pdr and 20-mm weapons.

By 1943–44 the cruisers had become completely outclassed and were obsolete. The *Dragon* was loaned to the Polish Navy in exile in 1943 but was returned to the RN in 1944 and replaced by the *Danae* which was renamed *Conrad.* The *Dragon* and *Durban* were both used as breakwaters for the invasion of the Normandy beaches in 1944. *Despatch* was disarmed and used as a depot ship but was given additional A/A armament.

Apart from *Dragon* and *Durban* expended at Normandy the only other *D* class cruiser lost was the *Dunedin* sunk by *U124* on 24 November, 1944. The rest of the class were scrapped between 1946–48.

*Durban. Authors Collection*

*Dragon* in 1919 with aircraft hangar under bridge. *P.Vicary*

# E Class
## *Emerald, Enterprise**

Having designed the *C* and *D* class cruisers on the basis (subsequently found to be untrue) that Germany was building more powerful cruisers, then it was in a way only natural that Britain should try to keep one-step-ahead of her adversary. Thus the *E* class was designed in anticipation that Germany might design a new class of cruiser superior to the British *C* and *D* classes. The overriding requirement was high speed, for light cruisers sacrificed protection and armament to achieve high speed. Therefore the *E* class had to be capable of speeds higher than any that might be developed by the Germans. This resulted in a Staff Requirement in which the whole design of the *E* class was based on the need to achieve a speed of 32 knots at full load displacement.

To achieve this extra 4 knots in speed over the previous *D* class much more powerful machinery had to be installed, which in turn necessitated an increase in length by 100-ft. This gave a much improved length: beam ratio which in turn led to better hydrodynamic performance. Unfortunately displacement was increased by over 50 per cent by these features and as a result the armament that the *E* class could mount was little better than that fitted to the D class: all this to achieve just an extra four knots in speed.

To achieve the higher speed there had to be sacrifices, which mainly centred on the armament. Only one extra 6-in gun could be mounted, and torpedo armament remained the same as in the *D* class. The arcs of fire from certain guns was improved by resiting them while the *Enterprise* was fitted with an experimental twin turret in 'A' position.

Freeboard was slightly increased to improve sea-keeping qualities and enable the vessels to maintain high speeds in adverse weather conditions.

The machinery arrangement differed considerably from the previous classes of light cruiser as a result of the need to install greater power. The number of shafts was doubled and two extra boilers fitted: the shaft horsepower was in fact doubled over that of the *D* class.

The ships were up-dated in 1934–36 and an aircraft catapult fitted instead of the flying off platforms previously carried. Offensive capability was enhanced by replacing the four triple torpedo mounts with quadruple mounts.

Although by 1939 this was a somewhat dated design the two cruisers (*Euphrates* was cancelled in 1919) were, nevertheless, powerful units with a high turn of speed. The light A/A was generally improved during the war, some of the beam 6-in being replaced with multiple 2-pdr weapons. A number of 20-mm were also added while the after banks of torpedo tubes were removed. Radar was also fitted.

The two cruisers were generally employed on convoy protection during the war and were sold for scrap post war.

*Enterprise* in 1925. *Tom Molland*

*Enterprise* after an action in the Bay of Biscay in December 1943. Note the gunnery and air warning radar. *IWM*

## Leander Class

### *Achilles*, Ajax, Hobart (ex-Apollo), Leander, Neptune, Orion, Perth (ex-Amphion), Sydney (ex-Phaeton)**

With the opening of the London Naval Conference in 1930 Britain made it clear that she would not be continuing construction of heavy cruisers. The outcome of the conference was to ban further construction of 8-in gunned 10,000 ton cruisers and under the terms Britain would be allowed to build up to 91,000 tons of light cruisers during the period of the Treaty (i.e. up to 1936).

Discounting Italian light cruiser designs which had been developed to counter the French Super Destroyers, the Royal Navy designed a light cruiser in answer to the German ***Königsberg*** class. The design parameter were prescribed by the requirement that the ships should carry light 6-in guns in twin mounts and be capable of speeds of 32 knots.

A number of features of the *Exeter* were incorporated into the new design — length of foc's'le deck, grouping of secondary armament, arrangement of machinery spaces. In fact with improved boilers which were stipulated it was found that only six were required (there were eight in *Exeter*) and the exhausts were therefore trunked into a single distinctive funnel.

The twin turret was developed from the experimental model tested in the *Enterprise*, and the gun was capable of 60 degree elevation.

A similar, but improved, scheme of protection to that in the *Exeter* was adopted for the new class. Even so the class can be generally considered to have had insufficient and inadequate protection, except in the area of the magazines and machinery spaces.

The *Phaeton, Apollo* and *Amphian* transferred to the RAN in 1935 and renamed respectively *Sidney* (1935), *Hobart* (1938) and *(Perth)* (1939), were completed to a modified design, with the engine and boiler rooms being sited in a combined unit with only four boilers (larger than those in the other ships); the forward unit driving the outer shafts and the after unit the inner shafts. This system greatly reduced the probability of immobility resulting from battle damage. This resulted in the vessels being given two widely spaced funnels.

The new machinery arrangement necessitated resiting the catapult which was moved from its position forward of the after superstructure to a position between the two funnels.

Surviving units received substantial additions to their light A/A during the war, with up to seven 40-mm, and 13×20-mm being added.

*Neptune* was mined off Tripoli, *Sydney* was sunk by the German AMC *Kormoran* in the Pacific, and *Perth* sunk by Japanese surface forces in the Sunda Straits.

*Ajax. A & J Pavia*

*Apollo* in October 1934. *P.Vicary*

*Achilles. Real Photographs*

*Perth.* Note two widely spaced funnels. *Real Photographs*

## Arethusa Class
## *Arethusa, Aurora*, Galatea, Penelope*

The design requirement for this class requested a light cruiser suitable for trade protection duties to be built to the minimum size, armament and protection to be consistent with this requirement.

When completed the design showed many of the characteristics of the *Amphion* in the preceeding class. The major difference was the omission of X turret and a corresponding reduction in length of some 50-ft to reduce displacement. The general lack of space topsides resulted in the siting too close together of the secondary battery and the possibility of carrying only triple torpedo tube mounts instead of the quadruple mountings of the previous class.

Extensive use of electric welding in this class (the *Arethusa* was the first British cruiser so constructed) did much to contain the weight problem.

*Aurora* and *Penelope* were completed to a slightly different design to improve the A/A arcs of fire, the 4-in guns being sited in twin mountings instead of single mounts as in the previous class.

The *Aurora* lacked the aircraft and catapult of the other units, the space being used to provide extra accommodation to enable her to act as a flagship.

During the war extra light A/A (two quadruple 40-mm and up to nine single 20-mm) was added together with various radars.

The cruisers were extensively employed in the Mediterranean during the war, *Galatea* being sunk off Alexandria by *U557* and *Penelope* off Anzio by *U410*.

*Penelope. Real Photographs*

*Aurora. Real Photographs*

## Town Class

### *Belfast*, Birmingham, Edinburgh*, Glasgow†, Gloucester, Liverpool†, Manchester†, Newcastle (ex-Minotaur), Sheffield, Southampton (ex-Polyphemus)*

This class was developed from a triple turret design of the *Amphion*, but considerably enlarged to carry a much heavier armament and protection. A hangar had been found to be essential to maintain the aircraft in a serviceable condition and this was a major staff requirement for the design. The siting of the hangar and its subsequent affect on the design gave rise to a sizeable superstructure forward. The final design therefore showed a little resemblance to the *Amphion* and so it was decided to name the class after major British towns.

The armament and its disposition was a major feature of the design requirement. The calibre chosen was the same 6-in (152-mm) as carried by the *Amphion*, but mounted in four triple turrets, thereby increasing the number of guns by four. Secondary armament consisted of eight twin 4-in (100-mm) mounts sited on either beam just abaft the after funnel. The hangar was an extensive structure housing two Walrus amphibians sited on either side of the fore funnel immediately forward of the thwartships catapult. To house the Walrus the hangar had to be increased in height over the original design which led to the bridge, which extended forward of the hangars being raised by one deck and the funnel height increased with a sharp rake to carry exhaust fumes well away from the bridge area. The light A/A was mounted atop the hangar to provide A/A coverage forward.

Protection was improved over that in the *Amphion* with the armoured belt along the waterline increased in length.

The second (*) and third (†) group differed slightly from the first. In the second group the bridge was completed with a semi-circular front and the gunnery fire control improved. In the third group certain parts of the design and internal arrangements were modified and protection and secondary armament improved.

The class was probably the most extensively used of any of the British cruisers during the war, serving in all theatres of operation. Numerous alterations, especially to the light A/A armament, were affected. This was expanded early in the war by the addition of between six and nine single 20-mm. Later in the war X turret was removed and the A/A further augmented, the ships carrying varying outfits of 8, 16 or 26 multiple 2-pdrs, 16 to 18 40-mm and 12 to 18 20-mm, while on *Belfast* the two after twin 4-in mounts were removed.

The *Belfast* was severely damaged by a mine early in the war and underwent extensive repairs. Of the rest of the class the *Southampton* had to be scuttled in the Mediterranean after being severely damaged by German and Italian aircraft; *Gloucester* was similarly sunk off Crete; the *Manchester* was sunk by Italian MTBs off Tunisia; and *Edinburgh* was sunk by *U456* and the German destroyers *Z24* and *Z25* in the Barents Sea.

*Belfast.* *Real Photographs*

*Sheffield* as completed. *Real Photographs*

*Edinburgh.* *Real Photographs*

*Manchester* as completed. *Real Photographs*

A wartime shot of *Sheffield.* *IWM*

## Dido Class

*Argonaut, Bellona*, Black Prince*, Bonaventure, Charybdis, Cleopatra, Diadem*, Dido, Euryalus, Hermione, Naiad, Phoebe, Royalist*, Scylla, Sirius, Spartan**

Once the Naval Treaties had lapsed and Britain was free to re-arm the main consideration was to improve the Navy's strength in the cruiser category, this having suffered severely, not only in numbers but also in design limitations. Two options were open, one to build a small updated version of *Arethusa* type, the other to develop the original *Town* class into a new design.

The former option was chosen as it would enable more cruisers to be built and thus make up for the lack of numbers. The same basic hull design and machinery plant as the *Arethusa* was chosen (thus saving time in not having to prepare a completely new design and develop new machinery) so modified as to mount a new type and style of armament. It was decided that as the ordnance factories had been so run down in the inter-war period a gun already under development would have to be selected for the new cruisers. It was settled that the ships should be designed to perform a dual role of A/A and surface warfare and to this end it was decided that they should retain the 10 gun armament of the *Arethusa*, but that it would be a single calibre. The 5.25-in (133-mm) DP weapon then being fitted to the *King George V* battleships was chosen. Unfortunately the required dual role led to a somewhat diminished capability for the fire control equipment and gun mounting had thus to be necessarily complicated.

Internally the ships had to be re-designed to enable the magazines to be re-located in a more advantageous position for supplying the guns sited in three turrets forward, superimposed, and two aft. Further problems arose over the supply of 5.25-in mountings and *Phoebe* and *Dido* lacked Q turret and *Bonaventure* X turret, single 4-in guns being carried instead. These were subsequently replaced by 5.25-in mounts. For the same reason *Charybdis* and *Scylla* were completed with four twin 4.5-in (114-mm) guns in lieu of the 5.25-in which were fitted later.

The second group (*) deliberately omitted the third mounting, having a quadruple 2-pdr gun in its place. They further differed in having straight masts and funnels instead of the raked structures of the first group.

Numerous light A/A and radar were added during the war, up to 12×40-mm in quadruple mounts and between 12 and 16 20-mm.

*Naiad* was sunk off Crete by *U565*; *Bonaventure* by the Italian submarine *Ambra* off Sollum; *Hermione* off Sollum by *U205*; *Charybdis* off the north coast of France by *T23* and *T27*; and *Spartan* by German aircraft off Anzio. *Bellona* and *Black Prince* were loaned to the RNZN in 1948, *Bellona* being returned in 1956 and replaced by the *Royalist*.

*Scylla* as completed with four twin 4.5-inch mountings. *Real Photographs*

*Spartan* in wartime camouflage. Note the quadruple 2pdr and straight masts. *Real Photographs*

*Dido* with all five 5.25-inch mountings. *Real Photographs*

## Fiji Class

### *Bermuda, Ceylon*, Fiji, Gambia, Jamaica, Kenya, Mauritius, Newfoundland*, Nigeria, Trinidad, Uganda**

These were the only British cruisers to be designed to the 8,000 limit set by the London Naval Treaty of 1936. They were built to the second option open to the Admiralty (see *Dido* class) and were basically a *Town* class cruiser built on an 8,000 ton hull, the necessary weight saving being achieved by reducing protection and limiting the size of the machinery. The reduction in size also led to very cramped accommodation, but the ships enjoyed a high reputation, serving with distinction during the war.

The system of box protection in the *Town* class cruisers was dispensed with so that a thinner belt could be fitted, but deck armour was increased both in the extent of its coverage and in thickness.

Horsepower was reduced by 10,000-shp, but as the ship was lighter, speed was slightly better than in the *Town* class.

Numerous additions in the form of A/A and radar were effected during the war, all adding to the topweight. This increased to such an extent that the last three units — *Ceylon, Newfoundland* and *Uganda* — omitted X turret and the aircraft and its facilities. The rest of the class were similarly modified, except for *Gambia* and *Nigeria* which retained X turret. By the end of the war the light A/A was composed of between 8 to 20×2-pdr and 18 to 20×20-mm. *Kenya* lacked the 20-mm and 2-pdr but carried instead 18×40-mm. *Bermuda* and *Uganda* carried in addition to the 2-pdr and 20-mm, 4–8×40-mm.

*Gambia* was loaned to the RNZN between 1943–46, but was then returned. *Fiji* was sunk by German and Italian aircraft off Crete, while *Trinidad* was severely damaged by German aircraft in the Barents Sea and subsequently scuttled by the destroyer *Matchless*.

*Black Prince* with the Pacific Fleet. *Authors Collection*

*Cleopatra.* *Real Photographs*

*Sirius.* *Real Photographs*

*Jamaica* in wartime camouflage. Note the perspex cover to the radar aerial in front of the bridge and the gunnery radar atop the main director.
*Real Photographs*

*Bermuda* in wartime camouflage.
*Tom Molland*

*Uganda. Real Photographs*

## Minotaur Class

*Bellerophon (ex-Tiger, ex-Blake)*, Blake (ex-Blake, ex-Tiger)*, Lion (ex-Defence)*, Minotaur, Superb*, Swiftsure, Tiger (ex-Bellerophon)**

These cruisers were basically a modified *Fiji* design, but with X turret and the aircraft arrangements omitted from the outset in favour of increased A/A armament, which comprised a twin 4-in (100-mm) and two multiple 2-pdr.

Work progressed at a fairly swift pace in the early stages, but as the war situation improved the pace became less urgent and by the end of the war only *Minotaur, Swiftsure* and *Superb* had been completed. *Defence* had been launched and the others were still on the slips. *Minotaur* was subsequently transferred to Canada. *Bellerophon* was cancelled and scrapped while *Blake, Lion* and *Tiger* were suspended and subsequently completed some years later to a modified design with completely new armament.

*Swiftsure. Real Photographs*

*Swiftsure. Real Photographs*

*Lion* (ex-*Defence*) lying uncompleted in Gareloch after the war. *P. Vicary*

*Lion* completing in the Tyne in 1960. *P. Vicary*

## Neptune Class
## *Hawke, Neptune*

These two cruisers were designed as an enlarged version of the *Fiji-Minotaur* type. Being larger (length was increased by some 100-ft and beam by 12-ft) there was little weight to spare to increase the thickness of armour, which, because of the increased dimensions, had to cover a larger area.

The main armament was the standard triple 6-in (152-mm) turret, and the ships were to have a secondary armament of six twin 4.5-in (114-mm) DP guns. Light armament was to have been 40-mm and 20-mm. The heavy secondary battery was disposed amidships, as in previous classes, with an extra mounting forward and aft. The design made no provision for aircraft facilities.

*Hawke* was in fact laid down, but was subsequently cancelled and the material on the slip broken up. *Neptune*, although authorised, was never in fact ordered and work on the ships was abandoned in favour of the following *Minotaur* class.

## Minotaur Class
## *Centurion, Edgar, Mars, Minotaur*

The concept for this class was developed from the earlier *Dido* class, when it had been realised that to be really effective both in the surface role and as an A/A cruiser, a heavier DP weapon was required. An added bonus gained with a heavy DP gun was that it would obviate the need to provide a heavy secondary A/A battery of 4-in (100-mm) or 4.5-in (114-mm) guns. The major difficulty in designing such a gun was in developing a really effective automatic system coupled with advanced fire control capable of obtaining a sustained, accurate, high rate of fire.

A further problem with a larger calibre weapon was that of providing sufficient space for magazine stowage, although the problem would not be quite so vexed if a single calibre weapon was selected. For reasons of space and weight it was finally decided to compromise and develop a 6-in (152-mm) DP gun rather than an 8-in (203-mm) weapon.

Work on developing the new weapon, which it was decided should be carried on a hull of similar design to that of the preceeding *Neptune*, was authorised. Work on the *Neptune* class then ceased to enable work on the *Minotaur* to proceed. The design provided for an armament disposition identical to that of the *Dido*, and contrary to previous argument, a mixed A/A battery of 3-in (76-mm), 40-mm and 20-mm was chosen. The 3-in was also to be a new gun and it was subsequently decided to standardise on a single calibre secondary A/A battery of eight twin 3-in in two groups. These were to be sited around the bridge and about the after superstructure. The new 6-in and 3-in were subsequently developed and when the *Minotaur* was cancelled were then allocated to the *Blake*, *Lion* and *Tiger*.

The machinery in the *Minotaur* was re-arranged from the previous unit system to an en-echelon arrangement so that the ships would be less vulnerable to battle damage.

Although the design had been prepared for the new class, economic restrictions led to the cancellation of the project and none of the vessels was ordered.

| CLASS | *BIRMINGHAM* | *C* |
|---|---|---|
| Displacement | 5,100 | 4,180–4,290 |
| **DIMENSIONS** | | |
| Metric | 141×15×4.8 | 137×13×4.5 |
| Imperial | 462¾×49¾×15¾ | 450×42¾×14¾ |
| **MACHINERY** | | |
| Unit/shafts | GT/2 | GT/2 |
| HP/speed | 25,000/25½ | 40,000/29 |
| Radius/speed | NA | 2,240/24 |
| Fuel | 1,412 | 935 |
| **PROTECTION** | | |
| Main belt | 35–76 (1½–3) | 35–76 (1½–3) |
| Upper deck | None | 25 (1) |
| Lower deck | None | 25 (1) |
| Turrets | 25 (1) | 25 (1) |
| **ARMAMENT** | | |
| Guns and torpedo tubes | 8×152 (8×1)<br>3×100 (3×1) | 5×152 (5×1) (not in *)<br>10×100 (10×1) (in * only)<br>8×100 (4×2) (in † only)<br>2×76 (2×1), 2 (*8)×2pdr (2×1, *1×8)<br>(4×2pdr (1×4)), 8×12.7 (2×4) (in † only)<br>8×533 (4×2) TT |
| Aircraft/catapults | None | None |
| Complement | 470 | 439 |

| CLASS | *CAVENDISH* | *D* | *E* |
|---|---|---|---|
| Displacement | 9,860 (*9,550) | 4,850 | 7,550–7,580 |
| **DIMENSIONS** | | | |
| Metric | 184.5×19.8×6.2 | 143.5(*144)×14×5 | 173.7×16.6×5.4 |
| Imperial | 605×65×20½ | 471 (*472½)×46½×16½ | 570×54½×18 |
| **MACHINERY** | | | |
| Unit/shafts | GT/4 | GT/2 | GT/4 |
| HP/speed | 65,000 (*58,000)/30½ (*29½) | 40,000/29 | 80,000/33 |
| Radius/speed | 5,400/14 | 2,300/27 | 3,850/20 |
| Fuel | 2,150–2,600 | 1,050 | 1,746 |
| **PROTECTION** | | | |
| Main belt | 25–62.5 (1½–2½) | 35–76 (1½–3) | 35–76 (1½–3) |
| Upper deck | 25–35 (1–1½) | 25 (1) | 25 (1) |
| Lower deck | 25–35 (1–1½) | 25 (1) | 25 (1) |
| Turrets | 25 (1) | 25 (1) | 25 (1) |
| **ARMAMENT** | | | |
| Guns and torpedo tubes | 5 (7)×190 (single, not in *)<br>*9×152 (9×1)<br>5 (4, *8)×100 (5/4×1, *4×2)<br>16 (*8)×2pdr (4 (*2)×4)<br>7 (8)×20 (not in *)<br>12×12.7 (3×4) in * only<br>4×533 (4×1) TT | 6×152 (6×1)<br>3×100 (3×1)<br>2×2pdr (2×1)<br>12×533 (4×3) TT | 7×152 (7×1, *1×2+5×1)<br>3×100 (3×1)<br>2×2pdr (2×1)<br>16×533 (4×4) TT |
| Aircraft/catapults | None | None | 1/1 |
| Complement | 712 | 450 | 572 |

| CLASS | *LEANDER* | *ARETHUSA* | *TOWN* | *DIDO* |
|---|---|---|---|---|
| Displacement | 6,985–7,270 | 5,220–5,270 | 9,100–10,260 | 5,600–5,950 |
| **DIMENSIONS** | | | | |
| Metric | 169×17×6 | 154.2×15.5×5.1 | 180.2 (*187)×18.9 (*19.7)×6 | 156×15.4×5.2 (*5.6) |
| Imperial | 554¼×55¾×19¾ | 506×51×16¾ | 591½ (*613½)×62 (*64¾)×20 | 512×50½×17¼ (*18½) |
| **MACHINERY** | | | | |
| Unit/shafts | GT/4 | GT/4 | GT/4 | GT/4 |
| HP/speed | 72,000/32½ | 64,000/32¼ | 75,000 (*80,000)/32 (*32¼) | 62,000/33 |
| Radius/speed | 7,000/14 | NA | 6,000/14 | 4,240/16 |

| | | | | |
|---|---|---|---|---|
| Fuel | 1,800 | 1,325 | 1,950–2,250 | 1,100 |
| **PROTECTION** | | | | |
| Main belt | 100 (4) | 70 (2¾) | 114 (4½) | 76 (3) |
| Upper deck | 32 (1¼) | 25 (1) | 38 (1½) | 25 (1) |
| Lower deck | 32–38 (1¼–1½) | 25 (1) | 32–38 (1¼–1½) | 25–50 (1–2) |
| Turrets | 25 (1) | 25 (1) | 25–50 (1–2) | 25–38 (1–1½) |
| **ARMAMENT** | | | | |
| Guns and torpedo tubes | 8×152 (4×2)<br>8 (*4)×100 (4×2, *4×1)<br>12×12.7 (3×4)<br>8×533 (2×4) TT | 6×152 (3×2)<br>8×100 (4×2)<br>8×12.7 (2×4)<br>6×533 (2×3) TT | 12×152 (4×3)<br>8 (*12)×100 (4 (*6)×2)<br>8 (*16)×2pdr (2×4) (*2×8)<br>8×12.7 (2×4)<br>6×533 (2×3) TT | 10 (*8)×133 (5 (*4)×2)<br>8 (*12)×2pdr (2 (*3)×4)<br>8×12.7 (2×4) (not in *)<br>12×20 (6×2) in * only<br>6×533 (2×3) TT |
| Aircraft/catapults | 1/1 | 1/1 (not in *) | 2/1 | None |
| Complement | 570 | 500 | 750 (*850) | 480 (*530) |

| CLASS | *FIJI* | *MINOTAUR* | *NEPTUNE* | *MINOTAUR* |
|---|---|---|---|---|
| Displacement | 8,525–8,875 | 8,800–8,885 | 15,700 | 15,280 |
| **DIMENSIONS** | | | | |
| Metric | 170×18.9×6.2 | 170×19.2 (*19.5)×6.4 | 201.7×23.2×7.5 | 198×22.8×7.3 |
| Imperial | 555½×62×20½ | 555½×63 (*64)×21¼ | 662×76×24¾ | 650×75×24 |
| **MACHINERY** | | | | |
| Unit/shafts | GT/4 | GT/4 | GT/4 | GT/4 |
| HP/speed | 72,500/33 | 72,500/32½ | 108,000/33 | 100,000/32¼ |
| Radius/speed | 5,850/16 | 8,000/16 | 7,500/20 | 6,400/20 |
| Fuel | 1,700 | 1,850 | 2,850 | 2,300 |
| **PROTECTION** | | | | |
| Main belt | 82–89 (3¼–3½) | 82–89 (3¼–3½) | 38 (1½) | 32–89 (1¼–3½) |
| Upper deck | 50 (2) | 50 (2) | 38 (1½) | None |
| Lower deck | 32–50 (1¼–2) | 32–50 (1¼–2) | 25–38 (1–1½) | 38 (1½) |
| Turrets | 25–50 (1–2) | 25–50 (1–2) | 50–100 (2–4) | 38–100 (1½–4) |
| **ARMAMENT** | | | | |
| Guns and torpedo tubes | 12 (*9)×152 (4(*3)×3)<br>8×100 (4×2)<br>8 (*16)×2pdr (2(*4)×4)<br>16×12.7 (4×4) (not in *)<br>20×20 (10×2) (in * only)<br>6×533 (2×3) TT | 9×152 (3×3)<br>10×100 (5×2)<br>16×2pdr (4×4)<br>6×40 (6×1)<br>6×533 (2×3) TT | 12×152 (4×3)<br>12×114 (6×2)<br>20×40 (10×2)<br>28×20 (14×2)<br>16×533 (4×4) TT | 10×152 (5×2)<br>6×76 (3×2)<br>20×40 (10×2)<br>32×20 (16×2)<br>16×533 (4×4) TT |
| Aircraft/catapults | 2/1 (not in *) | None | None | None |
| Complement | 920 | 960–1,000 | 1,351 | 1,282 |

| NAME | BUILDER | IN SERVICE | FATE | NAME | BUILDER | IN SERVICE | FATE |
|---|---|---|---|---|---|---|---|
| Achilles | 10 | 1933 | Trf India, *Delhi* 1948, BU 1979 | Curlew | 2 | 1917 | Lost 1/6/41 |
| Adelaide | 12 | 1922 | BU 1949 | Danae | 2 | 1918 | BU 1948 |
| Ajax | 46 | 1935 | BU 1949 | Dauntless | 33 | 1918 | BU 1946 |
| Arethusa | 11 | 1935 | BU 1950 | Delhi | 2 | 1919 | BU 1948 |
| Argonaut | 10 | 1942 | BU 1955 | Despatch | 16 | 1922 | BU 1946 |
| Aurora | 36 | 1937 | Trf China 1948, BU 1955 (?) | Diadem | 22 | 1944 | Trf Pakistan, *Babur* 1956 |
| Belfast | 21 | 1939 | Museum ship 1971 | Dido | 10 | 1940 | BU 1957 |
| Bellerophon | 47 | — | Canc 3/46 | Diomede | 45 | 1922 | BU 1946 |
| Bellona | 16 | 1943 | BU 1959 | Dragon | 39 | 1918 | Expended 8/7/44 |
| Bermuda | 23 | 1942 | BU 1965 | Dunedin | 2 | 1919 | Lost 24/11/44 |
| Birmingham | 15 | 1937 | BU 1960 | Durban | 39 | 1921 | Expended 9/6/44 |
| Black Prince | 21 | 1943 | BU 1962 | Edinburgh | 43 | 1939 | Lost 2/5/42 |
| Blake | 16 | 1961 | | Effingham | 36 | 1925 | Sc 21/5/40 |
| Bonaventure | 39 | 1940 | Lost 31/3/41 | Emerald | 2 | 1926 | BU 1948 |
| Cairo | 10 | 1919 | Lost 12/8/42 | Enterprise | 23 | 1926 | BU 1946 |
| Calcutta | 2 | 1919 | Lost 1/6/41 | Euryalus | 11 | 1941 | BU 1959 |
| Caledon | 12 | 1917 | BU 1948 | Fiji | 23 | 1940 | Lost 22/5/41 |
| Calypso | 22 | 1917 | Lost 12/6/40 | Frobisher | 15 | 1924 | BU 1949 |
| Capetown | 10 | 1922 | BU 1946 | Galatea | 39 | 1935 | Lost 15/12/41 |
| Caradoc | 39 | 1917 | BU 1946 | Gambia | 43 | 1942 | BU 1968 |
| Cardiff | 16 | 1917 | BU 1946 | Glasgow | 39 | 1937 | BU 1958 |
| Carlisle | 16 | 1918 | CTL 9/10/43 | Gloucester | 15 | 1939 | Lost 22/5/41 |
| Ceres | 23 | 1917 | BU 1946 | Hawke | 36 | — | Canc 3/46 |
| Ceylon | 42 | 1943 | Trf Peru, *Coronel Bolognesi* 1959 | Hawkins | 11 | 1919 | BU 1947 |
| Charybdis | 10 | 1942 | Lost 23/10/43 | Hermione | 42 | 1941 | Lost 16/6/42 |
| Cleopatra | 22 | 1941 | BU 1958 | Hobart | 15 | 1936 | BU 1962 |
| Colombo | 16 | 1919 | BU 1948 | Jamaica | 46 | 1942 | BU 1962 |
| Coventry | 43 | 1918 | Lost 14/9/42 | Kenya | 42 | 1940 | BU 1962 |
| Curacao | 34 | 1918 | Lost 2/10/42 | Leander | 15 | 1933 | BU 1950 |
| | | | | Liverpool | 16 | 1938 | BU 1958 |

| NAME | BUILDER | IN SERVICE | FATE |
|---|---|---|---|
| Lion | 39 | 1960 | BU 1972 |
| Manchester | 22 | 1938 | Lost 13/8/42 |
| Mauritius | 43 | 1940 | BU 1965 |
| Minotaur | 21 | 1945 | Trf Canada, *Ontario* 1945, BU 1960 |
| Naiad | 22 | 1941 | Lost 11/3/42 |
| Neptune i | 36 | 1934 | Lost 19/12/41 |
| Neptune ii | — | — | Projected |
| Newcastle | 47 | 1937 | BU 1949 |
| Newfoundland | 43 | 1942 | Trf Peru, *Almirante Grau* 1959 |
| Nigeria | 47 | 1940 | Trf India, *Mysore* 1957 |
| Orion | 15 | 1934 | BU 1949 |
| Penelope | 21 | 1936 | Lost 18/2/44 |
| Perth | 36 | 1936 | Lost 1/3/42 |
| Phoebe | 16 | 1940 | BU 1956 |
| Royalist | 39 | 1943 | BU 1968 |
| Scylla | 39 | 1942 | BU 1950 |
| Sheffield | 47 | 1937 | BU 1967 |
| Sirius | 36 | 1942 | BU 1956 |
| Southampton | 23 | 1937 | Sc 11/1/41 |
| Spartan | 46 | 1943 | Lost 29/1/44 |
| Superb | 43 | 1945 | BU 1960 |
| Swiftsure | 47 | 1944 | BU 1962 |
| Sydney | 43 | 1935 | Lost 19/11/41 |
| Tiger | 23 | 1959 | — |
| Trinidad | 15 | 1941 | Lost 15/5/42 |
| Uganda | 47 | 1943 | BU 1961 |
| Vindictive | 21 | 1918 | — |

# UNITED STATES

Midships detail of *Raleigh*. *Real Photographs*

## Omaha Class

### *Cincinnati*, Concord, Detroit*, Marblehead*, Memphis, Milwaukee, Omaha, Raleigh*, Richmond*, Trenton*

In designing this class of light cruiser (the first to be designed for the USN in over ten years) the Americans sought to improve on the best British and German World War I designs — the *D* and *Dresden* classes.

The design requirement laid down showed a vessel of 7,100 tons with a speed of 35 knots and an armament of eight 6-in (152-mm) guns.

The guns were mounted in armoured casemates on either beam fore and aft — two on either beam forward and two on either beam aft. To improve the broadside arcs of fire it was subsequently decided that the ships should mount two twin 6-in turrets, one forward and one aft. This resulted in a slightly adverse effect in other directions in that displacement was increased by 400 tons while speed fell by over a knot. Furthermore, in order that the displacement should not be increased too greatly, armour belt protection was reduced to just covering the machinery spaces. Further alterations to the original design which involved fitting torpedo tubes above the waterline (instead of submerged) and two catapults and aircraft led to half the class sacrificing two of the after casemate 6-in guns.

Few alterations were made to the vessels during the war. The aircraft and attendant facilities were removed and two quadruple 40-mm and about 14 single 20-mm mounts added together with radar. The class were all scrapped after the war.

*Omaha* in March 1939. *Marius Bar*

*Detroit* in 1923. *Marius Bar*

## Brooklyn Class

*Boise, Brooklyn, Helena*, Honolulu, Nashville, Philadelphia, Phoenix, St. Louis*, Savannah.*

This class was built in response to the Japanese *Mogami* (original design) class cruisers and the armament layout was inspired by that design. The Japanese considered that a cruiser mounting five triple 6-in (152-mm) turrets was more or less equal to a heavy cruiser mounting four twin 8-in (203-mm) i.e. the weight of the broadside delivered would be very similar, and so in poor visibility a light cruiser could work in closer to a heavier cruiser and deliver a higher rate of broadsides equalling or surpassing in weight those that could be fired by the heavy cruiser. This concept was certainly valid in pre-radar days.

The *Brooklyn* class was therefore designed with five triple turrets (three forward, two aft) and were flush decked with a high freeboard. Like other ships mounting three turrets forward, the third turret (which normally faced aft) suffered from limited arcs of training. The A/A was concentrated amidships and the aircraft facilities were sited well aft, the hangar (which could hold up to six floatplanes) being situated beneath the upper deck. Aircraft were brought up to the upper deck by lift and then placed by crane on one of the two catapults sited on the stern quarters. The large hangar gave rise to excessive vibration and from a damage point of view was considered to be a very vulnerable feature which was not repeated.

*Honolulu* in 1938 *Marius Bar*

Light A/A was increased during the war (four quadruple 40-mm and between 20–26 single 20-mm being added) and radar fitted. In the *Savannah* the single 5-in (127-mm) A/A mounts were removed and four twin 5-in DP added.

The only war loss suffered by the class was the *Helena* sunk by the Japanese destroyers *Suzukaze* and *Tanikaze* in the Kula Gulf. All but *Savannah* were transferred to South American navies after the war where some are still in service.

*St. Louis. Real Photographs*

## Atlanta Class
### *Atlanta, Juneau, San Diego*, San Juan**

Designed just before the outbreak of war these cruisers were much smaller than previous American light cruisers. With their heavy armament of A/A guns (16×5-in (127-mm)) which were fully capable of being used in surface action, these cruisers proved ideal for bolstering the strength of destroyer flotillas and were well capable of dealing with the heavily armed destroyers built by Japan during the war.

They suffered from a restricted radius of action, which was a severe penalty in the Pacific. This was brought about mainly from reduced bunkerage resulting from the reduction in displacement.

They were designed with a flush deck and considerable sheer forward to improve their sea-keeping qualities in the rough waters of the Pacific.

The armament of dual purpose 5-in guns should have made them a first class A/A cruiser but they suffered from having only two high-angle director control towers which severely limited the number of aerial targets which could be engaged at any one time.

Light A/A was improved during the war, the 1.1-in (28-mm) being replaced by four twin 40-mm and the addition of between 11 and 19 single 20-mm together with radar.

Two units were sunk during the war, the *Atlanta* in a night action with Japanese battleships at Guadalcanal and the *Juneau* by the submarine *I26*.

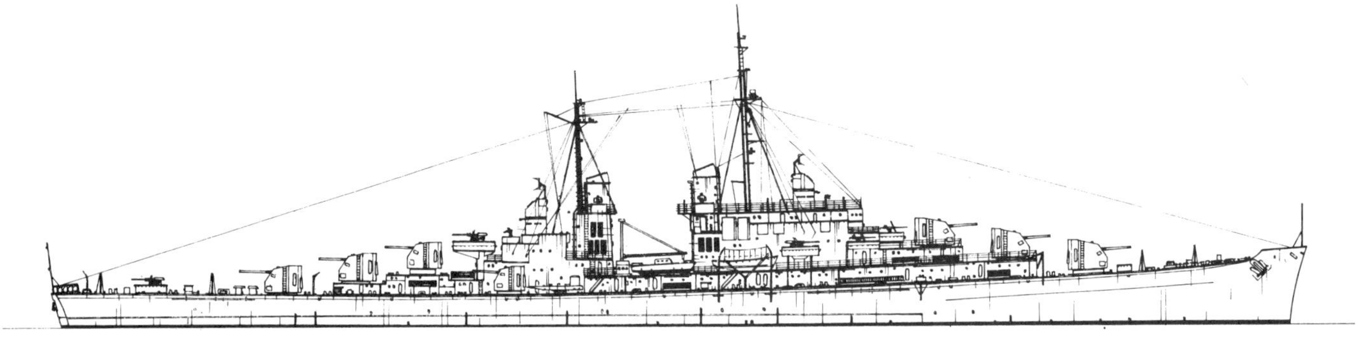

*CL-51 Atlanta*

## Cleveland Class

*Amsterdam (i), Amsterdam (ii), Astoria (ex-Wilkes Barre), Atlanta, Biloxi†, Birmingham, Buffalo, Cleveland*, Columbia*, Dayton (i), Dayton (ii), Denver†, Duluth, Fargo, Galveston, Houston (i), Houston (ii) (ex-Vicksburg)†, Huntingdon, Little Rock, Manchester, Miami, Mobile, Montpelier†, Newark, New Haven, Oklahoma City, Pasadena†, Portsmouth, Providence, Santa Fe†, Springfield†, Tallahassee, Topeka, Vicksburg (ex-Cheyenne), Vincennes (ex-Flint)†, Wilkes Barre, Wilmington, Youngstown, CL84, CL88.*

This was the largest class of cruisers ordered for the US Navy and were a development of the previous *Brooklyn* class sacrificing C turret in order to carry an extra twin 5-in (127-mm) DP mount.

Nine of the original units (*Amsterdam (i), Buffalo, Dayton, Fargo, Huntington, Newark, New Haven, Tallahassee, Wilmington*) were converted to carriers while on the stocks and were replaced by orders for a further nine units, three of which were cancelled.

They were wider in the beam than the later *Brooklyn* class, and the main belt at the waterline was shortened. Watertight integrity was considerably improved by a complete lack of openings in the hull, the ships being mechanically ventilated.

The heavy A/A armament of 5-in DP was well sited giving excellent arcs of fire, and the ships proved ideal as escorts for the fast carrier task forces in the Pacific.

During the war the A/A was continually improved by the addition of 40-mm, which eventually replaced the 20-mm, and radar both for warning and fire control.

None of the class was sunk during the war, although the *Birmingham* was severely damaged by an explosion on board the carrier *Princeton*, while the *Houston* suffered extensive damage after being struck by an aerial torpedo.

The class was obsolete by the 1950s and although some were converted to guided missile cruisers they were gradually relegated to the reserve and eventually scrapped.

*Pasadena.* *Real Photographs*

*Denver* in 1942. *Marius Bar*

*Providence* in 1948. *Marius Bar*

## Oakland Class
*Flint (ex-Spokane), Fresno*, Juneau (ii)*, Oakland, Reno, Spokane (ii)*, Tucson.*

This class was a development of the earlier *Atlanta* class in which the beam 5-in (127-mm) turrets were removed. The aim was to increase the number of light A/A and to this end triple torpedo tubes were mounted instead of the quad mountings of the *Atlanta* class; *Fresno, Juneau* and *Spokane* not carrying any torpedo tubes at all. Further these three cruisers carried B and X turrets at main deck level in order to reduce topweight even further, enabling even more A/A to be carried. They were designed from the outset to carry radar for air warning and gunnery control and even the 40-mm directors were fitted with radar.

Although the A/A concept was essential for the Pacific theatre of operations and the design in this respect proved adequate, it was found that the vessels were insufficiently armed, the weapons lacking the range and penetration capabilities of dealing with light surface units such as destroyers. The vessels suffered from a limited radius of action, brought about by the low bunkerage resulting from the overall limitation in displacement (they were the lightest cruisers in the US Navy).

*Flint* in wartime camouflage. *Real Photographs*

*Fresno.* *Real Photographs*

*Juneau* in 1948. *Real Photographs*

*Spokane* in April 1949. *Marius Bar*

## Fargo Class

*Buffalo, Chatanooga, Cheyenne, Fargo, Huntingdon (ii), Helena (ii), New Haven (ii), Newark, Roanoke, Tallahassee (ii), Vallejo, Wilmington (ii), CL115.*

This class was a modification of the *Cleveland* class in which the superstructure was redesigned in a more compact form to improve the arcs of fire of the A/A guns. In addition the boiler uptakes were trunked into a single funnel.

To reduce topweight and allow extra A/A to be mounted (quadruple 40-mm amidships), the two wing 5-in (127-mm) turrets were resited at main deck level. All the armament was provided with radar equipped directors, including the local directors for the 40-mm guns.

Modifications and alterations to the design so slowed construction that by the end of the war only two units had been launched while *Helena, Roanoke, Vallejo* and *CL115* had not even been laid down.

*Fargo* in April 1949. *Marius Bar*

## Worcester Class

*Gary, Roanoke (ii), Vallejo (ii), Worcester, CL154-159*

This design was a very enlarged version of the earlier *Oakland* class in which the 5-in (127-mm) DP turrets were replaced by fully automatic 6-in (152-mm) twin turrets. Displacement was considerably increased from 6,000 tons to 14,700 tons and length by 138 ft. A large part of the increased displacement was accounted for by the heavier armament. Protection was also increased (also adding to the displacement) the waterline belt being extended, and increased in thickness and depth. This increased displacement necessitated much more powerful machinery, which also added to the overall increase in weight of equipment.

The design embodied all the war experience accumulated to date with a reasonably powerful main armament backed up by a well balanced A/A armament of 3-in (76-mm) guns, which replaced the mixed calibre of 5-in, 40-mm and 20-mm carried by other cruisers.

The design was probably the ultimate in light cruiser design and the ships were powerful, well protected vessels, but as in all designs there had to be a sacrifice. In this case it was the considerable increase in displacement.

Only two of the cruisers had been laid down by the time the war ended, and the remainder were subsequently cancelled.

| CLASS | *OMAHA* | *BROOKLYN* | *ATLANTA* | *CLEVELAND* |
|---|---|---|---|---|
| Displacement | 7,050 | 9,475–10,000 | 6,000 | 10,000 |
| **DIMENSIONS** | | | | |
| Metric | 169.3×16.84×6 | 185.3×18.8×7.3 | 165×16.2×8 | 185.8×20.3×7.6 |
| Imperial | 555½×55¼×20 | 608¼×61¾×24 | 541½×53¼×26½ | 610×66½×25 |
| **MACHINERY** | | | | |
| Unit/shafts | GT/4 | GT/4 | GT/4 | GT/4 |
| HP/speed | 90,000/33¾ | 100,000/32½ | 75,000/33 | 100,000/33 |
| Radius/speed | | | | |
| Fuel | 2,068 | 2,084–2,207 | 1,435 | 2,415–2,620 |

| | | | | |
|---|---|---|---|---|
| **PROTECTION** | | | | |
| Main belt | 76 (3) | 38–127 (1½–5) | 89 (3½) | 38–127 (1½–5) |
| Upper deck | 38 (1½) | None | None | None |
| Main deck | None | 76 (3) | 50 (2) | 76 (3) |
| Lower deck | 38 (1½) | 64 (2½) | 50 (2) | 50 (2) |
| Turrets | 25–50 (1–2) | 76–127 (3–5) | 25–38 (1–1½) | 76–127 (3–5) |
| Conning tower | None | 165 (6½) | 95 (3¾) | 165 (6½) |
| **ARMAMENT** | | | | |
| Guns and torpedo tubes | 12 (*10)×152/53 (2×2+8(*6)×1)<br>8×76/50 (8×1)<br>2×3pdr (2×1)<br>8×12.7 (8×1)<br>6×533 (2×3) TT | 15×152/47 (5×3)<br>8×127/25 (8×1, *4×2)<br>4×3pdr (4×1)<br>8×12.7 (8×1) | 16×127/38 (8×2)<br>8×20 (8×1) in * only<br>8×533 (2×4) TT | 12×152/47 (4×3)<br>12×127/38 (6×2)<br>(28 (*8, †24)×40 (4×4+6×2, †4×4+4×2)<br>10–21×20 (singles) |
| Aircraft/catapults | 2/2 | 2/4 | None | 2/4 |
| Complement | 458 | 1,200 | 810 | 1,426 |

| CLASS | *OAKLAND* | *FARGO* | *WORCESTER* |
|---|---|---|---|
| Displacement | 6,000 | 10,000 | 14,700 |
| **DIMENSIONS** | | | |
| Metric | 165×16.2×8 | 186.2×20.3×7.6 | 207×21.5×7.6 |
| Imperial | 541½×53¼×26½ | 611¼×66½×25 | 679½×70¾×25 |
| **MACHINERY** | | | |
| Unit/shafts | GT/4 | GT/4 | GT/4 |
| HP/speed | 75,000/33 | 100,000/33 | 120,000/32¾ |
| Radius/speed fuel | 1,435–1,450 | 2,500 | 3,300 |
| **PROTECTION** | | | |
| Main belt | 89 (3½) | 38–127 (1½–5) | 76–152 (3–6) |
| Upper deck | None | None | None |
| Lower deck | 50 (2) | 76 (3) | 76 (3) |
| Turrets | 50 (2) | 50 (2) | 50 (2) |
| Conning tower | 25–38 (1–1½) | 76–127 (3–5) | 100 (4) |
| | 95 (3¾) | 165 (6½) | 165 (6½) |
| **ARMAMENT** | | | |
| Guns and torpedo tubes | 12×127/38 (6×2)<br>16 (*28)×40 (8×2, *4×4+6×2)<br>16 (*20)×20 (singles)<br>6×533 (2×3) TT, not in * | 12×152/47 (4×3)<br>12×127/38 (6×2)<br>28×40 (6×4+2×2)<br>28×20 (14×2) | 12×152/47 (6×2)<br>24×76/50 (11×2+2×1) |
| Aircraft/catapults | None | 2/4 | 1 helicopter |
| Complement | 820 | 1,200 | 1,700 |

*Worcester* in 1951. *Marius Bar*

| NAME | BUILDER | IN SERVICE | FATE |
|---|---|---|---|
| Amsterdam i | 31 | — | Completed as *CVL 22* |
| Amsterdam ii | 29 | 1945 | Str 1971 |
| Astoria | 13 | 1944 | Str 1969 |
| Atlanta i | 17 | 1941 | Lost 13/11/42 |
| Atlanta ii | 31 | 1944 | Str 1970 |
| Biloxi | 29 | 1943 | BU 1962 |
| Birmingham | 29 | 1943 | BU 1959 |
| Boise | 29 | 1938 | Trf Argentina, *Neuve de Julio*, 1951 |
| Brooklyn | 30 | 1935 | Trf Chile, *O'Higgins*, 1951 |
| Buffalo i | 31 | — | Completed as *CVL 29* |
| Buffalo ii | 31 | — | Canc 12/8/45 |
| CL84 | 17 | — | Canc 16/12/40 |
| CL88 | 17 | — | Canc 16/12/40 |
| CL115 | 31 | — | Canc 5/10/44 |
| Chatanooga | 29 | — | Canc 12/8/45 |
| Cheyenne | 29 | — | Canc 12/8/45 |
| Cincinnati | 44 | 1924 | BU 1946 |
| Cleveland | 31 | 1942 | BU 1960 |
| Columbia | 31 | 1942 | BU 1960 |
| Concord | 13 | 1923 | BU 1947 |
| Dayton i | 31 | — | Completed as *CVL 26* |
| Dayton ii | 31 | 1945 | BU 1962 |
| Denver | 31 | 1942 | BU 1960 |
| Detroit | 6 | 1923 | BU 1946 |
| Duluth | 29 | 1944 | Str 1960 |
| Fargo i | 31 | — | Completed as *CVL 27* |
| Fargo ii | 31 | 1945 | Str 1970 |
| Flint | 8 | 1944 | Str 1965 |
| Fresno | 17 | 1946 | BU 1964 |
| Galveston | 13 | 1958 | Re-rated *CLG3* 1956. Str 1973 |
| Gary | 31 | — | Canc 12/8/45 |
| Helena i | 30 | 1939 | Lost 13/11/42 |
| Helena ii | 31 | — | Canc 5/10/44 |
| Honolulu | 30 | 1938 | BU 1960 |
| Houston | 29 | 1943 | BU 1961 |
| Huntingdon i | 31 | — | Completed as *CVL 25* |
| Huntingdon ii | 31 | 1946 | BU 1962 |
| Juneau i | 17 | 1942 | Lost 13/11/42 |
| Juneau ii | 17 | 1946 | BU 1959 |
| Little Rock | 13 | 1945 | Str |
| Manchester | 7 | 1946 | BU 1961 |
| Marblehead | 13 | 1924 | BU |
| Memphis | 13 | 1925 | BU |
| Miami | 13 | 1943 | BU 1963 |
| Milwaukee | 44 | 1923 | Trf USSR ret 1945–6, BU |
| Mobile | 29 | 1943 | BU 1960 |
| Montpelier | 31 | 1942 | BU 1960 |
| Nashville | 31 | 1938 | Trf Argentina, *Captain Prat* 1951 |
| Newark i | 31 | — | Completed as *CVL 30* |
| Newark ii | 31 | — | Canc 12/8/45 |
| New Haven i | 31 | — | Completed as *CVL 24* |
| New Haven ii | 31 | — | Canc 12/8/45 |
| Oakland | 8 | 1943 | BU 1959 |
| Oklahoma City | 13 | 1944 | Str |
| Omaha | 44 | 1923 | BU |
| Pasadena | 7 | 1944 | Str 1970 |
| Philadelphia | 35 | 1937 | Trf Brazil, *Barroso* 1951 |
| Phoenix | 31 | 1938 | Trf Argentina, *Diecisiete de Octubre* 1951 |
| Portsmouth | 29 | 1945 | Str 1970 |
| Providence | 7 | 1945 | |
| Raleigh | 6 | 1924 | BU |
| Reno | 8 | 1943 | BU 1959 |
| Richmond | 13 | 1923 | BU |
| Roanoke i | 31 | — | Can 5/10/44 |
| Roanoke ii | 31 | 1949 | Str 1970 |
| St Louis | 29 | 1939 | Trf Brazil, *Tamandare* 1951 |
| San Diego | 7 | 1942 | BU 1959 |
| San Juan | 7 | 1942 | BU 1959 |
| Santa Fe | 31 | 1942 | BU 1960 |
| Savannah | 31 | 1938 | BU 1960 |
| Spokane | 17 | 1946 | Str |
| Springfield | 7 | 1944 | |
| Tallahassee i | 31 | — | Completed as *CVL 23* |
| Tallahasssee ii | 29 | — | Canc 12/8/45 |
| Topeka | 7 | 1944 | Str 1973 |
| Trenton | 13 | 1924 | BU |
| Tucson | 8 | 1945 | Str 1966 |
| Vallejo i | 31 | — | Canc 5/10/44 |
| Vallejo ii | 31 | — | Canc 12/8/45 |
| Vicksburg | 29 | 1944 | BU 1964 |
| Vincennes | 7 | 1944 | Str 1966 |
| Wilkes Barre | 31 | 1944 | Str 1971 |
| Wilmington i | 31 | — | Completed as *CVL 28* |
| Wilmington ii | 13 | — | Canc 12/8/45 |
| Worcester | 31 | 1948 | Str 1970 |
| Youngstown | 13 | — | Canc 12/8/45 |

## WORLD WAR 2 FACT FILES

This new series, prepared by experts who edit the world's foremost military, naval and aviation reference books, covers the fighting forces of the principal countries which took part in the Second World War. Each study provides a readable narrative supplemented by separate sections on technical details of weaponry that are seldom given in campaign and battle studies.

*Published:*

**AIRCRAFT CARRIERS**
**AXIS SUBMARINES**
**ALLIED SUBMARINES**
**AXIS CRUISERS**
**ANTI-TANK WEAPONS**
**MACHINE GUNS**
**BRITISH ESCORT SHIPS**
**AMERICAN GUNBOATS AND MINESWEEPERS**
**MORTARS AND ROCKETS**
**ANTI-AIRCRAFT GUNS**
**LIGHT AND MEDIUM FIELD ARTILLERY**
**SELF-PROPELLED ANTI-TANK AND ANTI-AIRCRAFT GUNS**
**HEAVY ARTILLERY**
**INFANTRY, MOUNTAIN AND AIRBORNE GUNS**
**AXIS PISTOLS, RIFLES AND GRENADES**
**ALLIED PISTOLS, RIFLES AND GRENADES**
**SUB-MACHINE GUNS AND AUTOMATIC RIFLES**
**AXIS COMBAT TANKS**
**ALLIED COMBAT TANKS**

WW2 Aircraft Fact Files

**U.S. NAVY AND MARINE CORPS FIGHTERS**
**JAPANESE ARMY AIR FORCE FIGHTERS (PARTS 1 AND 2)**
**SOVIET AIR FORCE FIGHTERS (PARTS 1 AND 2)**
**U.S. ARMY AIR FORCE FIGHTERS (PARTS 1 AND 2)**
**RAF FIGHTERS (PARTS 1 AND 2)**
**RAF BOMBERS (PARTS 1)**

*In preparation:*

**RAF FIGHTERS (PART 3)**
**RAF BOMBERS (PART 2)**